Neglected
Treasure

Rediscovering the Old Testament

Neglected Treasure

Rediscovering the Old Testament

by

Dan G. Johnson

BRISTOL BOOKS

NEGLECTED TREASURE
Rediscovering the Old Testament
Copyright 1989 by Dan G. Johnson
Published by **Bristol Books**

First Edition, April 1989

Library of Congress Card Number: 89-50312
ISBN: 0-917851-28-5
Suggested Subject Headings:
1. Bible—Old Testament
Recommended Dewey Decimal Classification: 221,'61

BRISTOL BOOKS
An imprint of Good News, A Forum for Scriptural Christianity, Inc.
308 East Main Street • Wilmore, Kentucky 40390

Contents

One

Rediscovering
the Treasure

Mel Fisher, persistent treasure hunter and entrepreneur, had been scouring the waters off Key West, Florida, for sixteen years in search of the famous treasure ship, Atocha. On July 20, 1987, forty miles offshore, his divers found the sunken ship and an incredible treasure worth four hundred million dollars. The sunken treasure, which he had pursued so vigorously, intentionally and persistently, had finally been discovered.

After fourteen years of ministry, I have come to the conclusion that the church has within its grasp a similar find—a treasure of infinitely greater value and worth. But, for the most part, we have failed to discover it. We have been far less vigorous, less intentional and less persistent in pursuing this treasure. I am speaking of the Old Testament, which I have come to regard as the "Neglected Treasure" of the church.

I believe this is true throughout the church. I have close friends in the ministry, each of whom is an effective pastor and gifted preacher, but they readily confess that they only rarely preach from the Old Testament. Even those individuals who follow the lectionary almost always choose the New Testament reading.

If the clergy of the church shy away from the Old Testament, how much more so do the laity. When I recently began a study series on the Old Testament in our church, several members told me that they really were not great fans of that portion of the Bible; in fact, they found it nearly impossible to comprehend, and what they did understand was often disturbing to them.

Such observations reflect the feelings of vast numbers of people in the church. It is unfortunate that anyone should view this portion of God's Word in such a manner because the Old Testament was indeed the sacred Scripture of the early church, and it continues to be the living Word of God that is authoritative and normative for our lives today. It is unnecessary because with only a little effort the Old Testament *can* be understood, and once understood, it will be immensely appreciated.

Unfortunately we often encounter some negative and erroneous perceptions about the Old Testament which must be corrected before we can proceed. Because of these aberrations the Old Testament has become the neglected treasure of the church. I will address six major culprits.

1. The Old Testament Is Law;
the New Testament Is Gospel

Martin Luther popularized this view in the sixteenth century, and it continues to be influential today. Luther incorrectly perceived a radical break between the *law* of the Old Testament and the *gospel* of the New Testament. The ripple effect has been extensive: the Old Testament is bad news, the New Testament is good news. The God of the Old Testament is a God of wrath and anger; the God of the New Testament is a God of love and compassion. The Old Testament is works; the New Testament is grace.

This view was first proposed in the second century by the heretic, Marcion, who advocated excising the Old Testament from the Canon. It was resurrected in sophisticated form at the turn of the twentieth century by the eminent German church historian, Adolf von Harnack. Following the philosophical lead of Georg W. F. Hegel, he concluded that the Old Testament was simply preparatory and that its time of importance had passed. More recently, the extraordinarily gifted German New Testament exegete and theologian, Rudolf Bultmann, writing in the Lutheran tradition, argued that the Old Testament is purely law and therefore of no theological value to the Christian.

To reduce the Old Testament to *law* is simply incorrect. For example, the call of Abraham to initiate the salvation history was a clear act of grace (Genesis 12). The great miracle of deliverance at the Red Sea, was surely a *gracious* act of God (Exodus 14). Likewise, is there a more powerful portrayal of the undeserved love of God than the emblematic story of Hosea and his wife, Gomer (Hosea 1, 2)? Dare we construe these dramatic examples of God's love as "bad news"? Or should we somehow see in them the attributes of a God of wrath and not a God of compassion? Is there indeed no grace in these sovereign acts of God? I think not. The law/gospel distinction simply will not stand.

2. The Old Testament Is Just History

The Old Testament, according to this view, contains the history of an ancient people, but just as Latin is now a "dead" language, so also the Old Testament is an obsolete, ancient history, so it is reasoned.

But the Old Testament is not simply history; it is *His Story,* God's Story. It is the dramatic portrayal of the ways in which God interacts with his people. And insofar as all human beings share a common essence and a common creature/Creator relationship, his story becomes *our story.*

Moreover, because of the way in which the Old Testament story is told, we are inexorably drawn into it. We are on Mt. Moriah with Abraham as he prepares to sacrifice his son, Isaac (Genesis 22). We are captivated by the contest on Mt. Carmel between Elijah and the prophets of Baal. *Our* need to choose whom we will serve forcefully bears down upon us as we hear Elijah's immortal words: "If the Lord is God, follow him; but if Baal is God, follow him" (1 Kings 18:21). (Or as Peter Marshall concluded a famous sermon text, ". . . if Baal be God, then serve him and go to hell!") With David we feel that surge of divine courage as he knelt to pick up the stones to sling at Goliath (1 Samuel 17). This is not dull, ineffectual history; this is the living Word of the living God!

Garrison Keillor, known by thousands of public radio listeners as the host of "The Prairie Home Companion" and author of the best seller, *Lake Wobegon Days*, is a modern-day Mark Twain, a storyteller par excellence. The most popular portion of his two-hour radio program (now in reruns) was a twenty-minute segment in which he captivated listeners by simply telling a story about life in the mythical village of Lake Wobegon.

Keillor, in a *Time* magazine cover story, related how he became interested in storytelling. As a young boy in Minnesota before the age of television, he would lie on the floor by the fireplace and listen to his uncle Len tell family stories by the hour. "It was this experience," he said, "that gave us a sense of who we were. We were not just chips floating aimlessly on the ocean. We had a sense of place."

It is this marvelous sense of place that the Old Testament has the capacity to give us. We have a history. And because we have a history, we have a present and a future. We belong; we are a part of a people of faith. Much of the instability that characterizes the present age derives from the fact that we have lost a sense of who we are; we have forgotten, never heard or neglected our important story.

3. There Are Thorny Problems in the Old Testament

Unfortunately this is true, and these "problems" should

be confronted with integrity and candor. Frankly, I am not certain they can all be resolved to our satisfaction, but I am convinced that we should never allow a few difficulties to detour us from delving into the depths of God's Word.

The vindictive nature of some of the psalms troubles some readers. In my own view, this should be seen as simply the psalmist's honest reflection of deep and powerful feelings. We need neither sanction nor condemn these feelings. Such utter honesty is characteristic of the psalms; they consistently express the true feelings which we ourselves have. Honest expression of emotions, modern psychologists affirm, is an essential part of the process for handling them in a healthy way. For the most part, these psalms move through anger and bitterness to faith, trust and hope. Rather than sanctioning vindictiveness, they are intended to provide a model for moving from anger to trust.

Note Psalm 109, a particularly difficult one. The psalmist has been attacked and asks God to strike his attacker:

> Appoint an evil man to oppose him; let an accuser stand at his right hand. When he is tried, let him be found guilty, and may his prayers condemn him. May his days be few; may another take his place of leadership. May his children be fatherless and his wife a widow. May his children be wandering beggars; may they be driven from their ruined homes. . . . May his descendants be cut off, their names blotted out from the next generation (vv. 6-10; 13).

Seldom will you find a more vitriolic attack than this! But read on—the writer is overcome with his plight: "For I am poor and needy, and my heart is wounded within me" (v. 22). He feels oppressed and overwhelmed. His attack indicates desperation. Note his cry for help in verse 26: "Help me, O Lord my God; save me in accordance with your love." Once he has vented his feelings of anger and made his plea for help, the writer is able to move on to an expression of trust:

> With my mouth I will greatly extol the Lord;
> in the great throng I will praise him.

11

For he stands at the right hand of the needy one,
to save his life from those who condemn him (vv. 30, 31).

Furthermore, in my view it is frequently appropriate
to "psychologize" these portions of the Psalms. By that I
mean we may often construe the "enemies" of Israel as our
own emotional enemies (e.g., fear, doubt, insecurity,
depression) and call upon God to "attack" them. In that
sense these psalms become an affirmation of trust.[1]

*Punishment that seems disproportionate to the
crime* is another problem. The story of the sin of Achan in
Joshua 7 may serve as a representative of the Old Testament stories in which the punishments seem to outweigh
the crimes. Joshua and his troops had just captured
Jericho. It was understood that all of the possessions of the
Canaanites were off limits to all Israelites. But Achan
disobeyed the ban, stole some of the items and hid them
among his possessions. This displeased the Lord, and the
effect was an internal weakening of Israel so that they
were no longer able to stand against the enemy. At the next
military encounter they were soundly defeated.

When Joshua inquired of the Lord regarding this, God
replied that the defeat had come because Israel had sinned
and broken covenant. Upon investigation Joshua discovered that Achan was the culprit. Achan *and his entire
family* were to be severely punished: "Then all Israel
stoned him, and after they stoned the rest, they burned
them" (v. 25).

On one reading, Achan simply took some items that he
had been forbidden to take. Such a crime surely did not
merit stoning, it may be argued. But on another reading,
Achan broke covenant with his God and with his people.
Like Ananias and Sapphira in the New Testament (Acts 5),
he acted deceitfully. In both instances the result was death.

The Hebrew verb used to characterize Achan's deceitful
act is *ma'al*, and it is used almost solely with acts of
infidelity, either to God or in marriage. In Joshua 7:1 it is
employed twice to emphasize the severity of the treachery.

REDISCOVERING THE TREASURE

The story of the sin of Achan serves to highlight the *seriousness* of such acts of infidelity, particularly as these acts affect one's relationships with God and with the community of faith.

One of the primary purposes of the Old Testament is to teach the present-day community of faith about those things which please or displease God (cf. 2 Timothy 3:16, "All Scripture [Old Testament] is God-breathed and is useful for teaching, rebuking, correcting and training in righteousness . . ."). In that framework, the purpose of Achan's story is to teach us about the importance of a trust relationship and the seriousness of betrayal of trust. That is the theological message, and as such, it is normative.

Should Achan have been punished by death? It is difficult, and perhaps inappropriate, for us in the twentieth century to answer that question for someone in the thirteenth century B.C. However, in the light of New Testament teaching, this punishment cannot be considered normative for today. The pattern that should be followed for similar Old Testament passages is this: penetrate to the theological message of the text and then judge the particular details in the light of New Testament teaching.

The seemingly divine instruction to kill innocent people in the conquest of Canaan also troubles people. This is a terribly difficult problem. I have read many attempts to explain, justify and rationalize it, but have not found any of them convincing. Was this indeed God's will? Or was it simply the projection of the people's will onto God?

Were the people mistaken in thinking God directed them to slaughter all the inhabitants? Was this a necessary step in the evolution of the ancient world and the Hebrew faith? It is clear from the subsequent history of Israel, particularly from the writings of the prophets, that the Canaanites who remained in Israel had a negative affect on the Hebrew religion, but certainly similar influences would have come from the surrounding countries. Besides, true faith is characterized by an *inner* strength rather than by an *outer* force which would overpower those who disagree with it. We cannot accept the thought that the end justifies the means.

My own view is that this commendation of the killing of innocent people is a perplexing mystery in Old Testament history. It causes thinking people to raise serious questions, and we should not insult their intelligence with assertions which deny the reality of the problem. It may well be the better part of wisdom to admit that we simply do not fully understand it and perhaps never will. Some aspects of our faith must uncomfortably remain shrouded in mystery. This is one.

4. Old Testament Stories Are Just Children's Stories

Most of us would agree that one of the highlights of our childhood Sunday school days was the reading of the powerful stories of David and Goliath, Samson and Delilah, Daniel in the Lions' Den and others. These are magnificent stories and should be a part of every child's background.

But something very subtle has taken place, unaware to most of us. We have begun to associate these stories strictly with our childhood Sunday school experiences. We have failed to realize that the Word of God has levels of meaning. Each level speaks to us at our particular stage of development. In short, the text grows with us and relates to us at whatever age we might be. But when we relegate Old Testament stories to the realm of children's stories we become incapable of comprehending the underlying and potent theological messages intended for us as adults. Most of us have never been encouraged to push through the story to its theological intention.

For example, we all know the story of Samson (Judges 14-16), who seemingly found his strength in his hair. As children we were captivated by his feats of power. We also sensed something ominous when he fell in love with

14

Delilah. Alas, she was able to trick him into revealing that the secret of his strength was in his hair. When she cut it he was left weak and disabled, a pitiful figure.

On the surface, this story seems to be dealing with the benefits of long hair. But when we press on we learn that it contains a profound theological message. We read that Samson had been dedicated at birth according to the Nazirite vow; he was a "Nazirite of God" (Judges 13:7). A portion of that sacred vow to God dictated that his hair should never be cut. It was from within that covenant relationship with God that Samson drew his unusual strength. The cutting of the hair, which had no effect in itself, symbolized the tragic fracturing of Samson's relationship with his God. The theological message is clear: this broken relationship resulted in the loss of Samson's strength.

If the church would persistently penetrate through the "child" stage of these magnificent stories, it could feast upon the theological riches that lie awaiting it.

5. The Old Testament Is Difficult to Understand

So what? So are the works of Shakespeare, Chaucer and Dante. Most great literature is difficult to understand. The Old Testament's treasures will not be discovered without effort—but no true treasure ever is. And surely there are ample supplies of commentaries, Bible dictionaries, modern translations and other tools with which to search out the treasure.

But, in fairness to the reader, there is one other factor that affects our reading of the Old Testament: the fact that it is written from the perspective of the Hebraic mind. Most of us in the Western world have been steeped in the Greek way of thinking. We tend to think abstractly, logically, rationally. The Hebrew mind was more concrete and earthy. It thought in pictures and stories. For example, if the Old Testament (written almost exclusively in Hebrew) wanted to describe the concept of "faith," it wouldn't describe it conceptually; it would tell a story—e.g., the story par excellence of faith, that of Abraham and Sarah. Actually, such a method is a wonderful way to go about it.

Contrast this to the New Testament (written in Greek). If it wished to convey the concept of "faith" it would give a definition: "Now faith is being sure of what we hope for and certain of what we do not see" (Hebrews 11:1). Both are helpful, but the story of Abraham and Sarah, in my view, is much easier to grasp.

As you read through the Old Testament you will encounter a host of these Hebrew stories. I hope the "foreign" way of looking at the world, this Hebrew frame of reference, will become more familiar to you, and that you will be delighted and inspired by it; that the vehicle of the *story* will become the conveyor of the theological message of God, for indeed that was its original intention. Remember, Jesus, a Hebrew, almost always taught by using stories.

6. The New Testament Is Important for the Church; i.e., the Old Testament Is No Longer Necessary

Underlying this mistaken notion is the fact that we simply have not spent time with this portion of God's Word. If we would take the time to understand it, we would realize how important and necessary the Old Testament is.

We like to read the New Testament. It's manageable. It's not too long. We can make sense of (most of) it. But the Old Testament seems too burdensome, too tedious, and so we leave it on the shelf, unread and unknown.

Even book publishers reinforce our prejudices. Have we not all seen a copy of *The New Testament and the Psalms*? The implication is that for the Christian only the New Testament and the Psalms are really important. This is a tragic misconception.

We must remember that the Old Testament was the Scripture of the early church. This is what Peter, James, John and the rest of the Christian community read when they gathered for prayers, fellowship and the breaking of bread. It was the Old Testament which Jesus used on the road to Emmaus in order to interpret to his friends all that had taken place regarding himself: "And beginning with Moses and all the prophets, he interpreted to them in all the Scriptures the things concerning himself" (Luke 24:27, RSV). In so doing, Jesus refers to the three portions which comprise the Old Testament: "Moses" is a reference to the books of Moses, or the Pentateuch (Torah); "the prophets" refers to the early and late prophets, from Joshua through Malachi (*Nevi'im*); "the scriptures" refers to the poetic Old Testament Scriptures, e.g., Psalms, Proverbs, Ecclesiastes (*Kethubim*). The point is clear: we cannot understand who Jesus is without the Old Testament.

All of the titles given to Jesus in the New Testament— Suffering Servant, Son of God, Son of Man, Messiah, the Prophet, High Priest, Lord, Savior and God—derive their meaning from the Old Testament. These titles, *in their Old Testament context,* are the keys to our understanding the character and ministry of Jesus, the Christ.

This ancient collection of books holds many of the keys to understanding our present and our future. In a 1986 cover story for *Time* magazine Roger Rosenblatt wrote a letter to people who would be living in the year 2086. The letter, placed in a time capsule inside the Statue of Liberty, was to be read on her two hundredth anniversary. He asks some delightful questions of his futuristic readers: "Do you still play baseball? Are there still such things as automobiles?" And then he suggests, "As you are jetting across the world, you may find, as we do, that you want to turn your seats *backward* in order to glean the wisdom of the past." It is time for us in the twentieth century to turn our seats backward and glean spiritual food from the neglected wisdom of the Old Testament, this treasure from the past that speaks so profoundly to us today.

Questions for Review

1. Have you ever been taught any of the six "erroneous perceptions" of the Old Testament mentioned in this chapter? Do you agree/disagree that they are erroneous?

2. Can you see how a characterization of the Old Testament as being "law with no grace" is incorrect? In addition to the examples cited in this chapter, can you think of other illustrations of God's grace and love in the Old Testament?

3. Far from being sterile, irrelevant history, the Old Testament is our story of faith. Think of various well-known Old Testament stories and reflect on how you are drawn into them as you read. Think, too, about the most effective preaching you have heard. Did it contain a significant portion of the vehicle of *story?*

4. You no doubt have been confronted by some of the "thorny problems" in the Old Testament. While they remain difficult to solve, persevere in grappling with them and do not allow them to keep you from the vast remaining portion of the Old Testament. As Mark Twain appropriately noted, "It's not the part of the Bible that I don't understand that gives me difficulty; it is the part that I *do* understand."

5. Once children have learned the Old Testament stories, is your church concerned about helping them as they grow in the faith to move deeper into the theological meaning of the story? Or does it stop short, thus reinforcing the impression that these are only children's stories?

6. Have you found the Old Testament difficult to understand? Do you feel that understanding the Hebraic way of thinking as described in this book will be an asset in your appreciation of the Old Testament?

TWO

Hosea Reaffirms God's Love

Vladimir Horowitz, world-renowned pianist, once played a little-known piano concerto by Beethoven for one of his students. When he finished he got up from the piano and sat down by the student. The student asked, "But what does it mean?"

Horowitz responded by returning to the piano and playing the piece again. "That's what it means," he said.

The ancient Hebrews communicated theological truth by telling a story, then by telling it again and again, from one generation to the next. They were marvelous storytellers, and while I make no claim to be on a par with them, I am aware of the inherent power of the story. Certainly this is true of the story of Hosea and his wife, Gomer. The story is so powerful and dramatic that I wish simply to retell the story and allow the message of God to speak through it. Sharpen your imaginative skills and come with me now to the Israelite town of Bethel.

The year is 753 B.C. It is early evening, and the western

sky is a brilliant multichromatic wonder. Hosea is sitting at home, basking in the beauty of God's creation. It has been a long and difficult day. The vineyards have been attended to—they would yield a good crop this year. Soon the time would come to bring in the harvest. The olive trees, too, looked better than usual. For young Hosea, life was good. He was grateful to the God who gave it.

He had felt closer to God in recent months. He couldn't explain it—just a closeness. And the services at the temple had meant more to him than they had in the past. There was a peace, a contentment, an added sensitivity to God that he had not previously known. Always before he had revered God, held him in awe. From childhood he had heard the stories of his people—how God led Abraham from a far off land to this land Hosea now called home. There were stories of Isaac and Jacob and Moses, the great one who delivered the children of Israel from Egypt. Then there were Joshua and Gideon and Deborah. They were all very important to him.

But lately there was something more going on—a strange inner stirring deep within his soul. He couldn't explain it. He didn't understand it. It was something like the excitement a young child has the night before her family makes a long trip—filled with anticipation.

And then it happened. That evening, as he sat watching the technicolor sky, Hosea thought he heard something—a voice, yes, it was an inaudible voice—speaking to him, calling him by name, "Hosea, Hosea."

It was the voice of God. "Hosea, I want you to be my child, my follower."

"Yes, Yahweh, I will."

But the voice came again, "Hosea, I want you to be my prophet, to speak to my people who have gone so disastrously astray. They no longer have any understanding of me. They obey other gods, and they are being ruined. I need a prophet, a spokesman, to go to them and bring them back to me. Hosea, will you be that person?" (author's paraphrase).

This was far more than Hosea had bargained for. He had a farm that was beginning to do well. His hard work was finally paying off. The future looked bright. But now God wanted him to become a prophet. He knew nothing about being a prophet. His father, Beri, was not even religious. What would he do? He knew enough about his religion, his God and the stories of his ancestors to know that the only viable option was to obey this call of God upon his life. So that evening, uneventful at first, evolved into a night that changed his life forever.

Not long afterward Hosea visited the marketplace in Bethel. Purchasing fruits and vegetables, his heart was heavy with this new-found calling, and his mind was consumed with the flagrant sins of his people. It seemed that the more sensitive he became to God and God's ways, the more aware he became of the lostness of his people. The more in tune he was with God, the more out of tune with God his people seemed to be.

At the market both his head and his heart felt heavy, when suddenly his thoughts were interrupted—interrupted by the wondrous sight of a beautiful young woman standing next to him, waiting to make purchases of her own. Her grace and poise reflected an inner beauty and charm that temporarily suspended all the other thoughts in Hosea's mind.

Her name, too, was beautiful. It was "Gomer," which in Hosea's Hebrew tongue means "completeness, fullness, perfection of beauty." She lived nearby and came to the market at the same hour three times a week. Hosea made a point to be there too. He quickly fell in love with Gomer and soon they were married. It was a joyous occasion. The festivities went on for a week. Then there were months of harmony and happiness, such that neither had known.

They had their first child, a son, and in the tradition of other prophets whose children were given names which carried special significance, Hosea named his firstborn son Jezreel, which means, "The destruction of Israel;" for if Israel did not repent, they would surely be destroyed.

What is it that causes the heart to wander? Quietly, slowly, Gomer began to change. Was it the responsibility of the new child? The long days and sleepless nights? Perhaps it was the loneliness Gomer felt with Hosea away so often prophesying in Dothan, Gilgal and Samaria. Whatever the reason, something happened inside the heart of Gomer. She began to be unfaithful, first with one man, then another and another.

At first Hosea was unsuspecting, though gradually he knew something was wrong. Then Gomer's waywardness became increasingly obvious. Rumors began to circulate around town. There was talk, and Hosea began to feel it as he made his way through the city. He could sense the stares at his back. The gossip weighed heavily upon him.

On those occasional evenings when Gomer was home, Hosea would plead with her, begging her to change her ways. She would—for a day or two. But then back to her pattern of infidelity she would go. The agony and heartbreak were almost unbearable, and many nights Hosea fell asleep on a tear-soaked pillow.

Their second child came, a beautiful daughter, and he called her "Lo Ruhamah" which means "not pitied" or "no compassion." It was a painfully appropriate name because Gomer had no compassion on Hosea. And further, this was a sign that God himself would have no compassion on the people Israel if they persisted in their self-destructive ways.

Just when Hosea thought Gomer could do no further damage to herself and to his heart, she made her way to the streets, standing in the doorways, offering herself to anyone who came by. She would come home infrequently— once or twice a month—enough to exacerbate the already penetrating pain which Hosea felt. She came home the final time to have her third child.

Hosea was given the task of naming this new baby. He chose the name "Lo Ami"—"not my people" or "not my child," for it was not his son, but the boy belonged to another. There was a broader meaning behind the name, an emblematic purpose for the name; it was God's way of saying to the people of Israel, "Lo Ami" or "You are not my people! You have forsaken me, you have left me, betrayed me. You have gone after other gods, sold yourselves to foreign deities and strange idols. You have forgotten who you are and whose you are, so you are no longer mine. You are no longer my people!"

And so, Hosea realizes that his fate with Gomer parallels that of God's relationship with Israel. Hosea's heartbreak with his wife Gomer is exactly like God's heartache over his people. Oh, how he loved Gomer in her youth, her dark and shiny hair, her beautiful skin, vibrant eyes, that inner beauty. How he cared for her, cherished her, spoke tenderly to her, gave himself for her. And she twisted his love and stamped on his affection, discarded his caring and brought him humiliation, shame and a broken heart.

In the same way God loved his people, called them as a young bride out of Egypt, nourished and cherished them through the desert, shed his affection upon them, cared for them. And his people twisted his love, stamped upon his affection, discarded his caring, turned away from this wonderful God of love and brought him humiliation, shame and a broken heart.

But come with me now to the final scene. We are again back to the marketplace, back where Hosea first laid eyes on his beautiful young bride; where he first felt the quickening of his heart as he gazed on her beauty and her charm. All had begun so delightfully well—here in the market place.

The locale is the same, but the circumstances are tragically different. Hosea's wayward wife, Gomer, is here too. But unlike that earlier time when she came to buy something at the market, she now has come to sell something.

She has come to sell herself as a slave; to sell her body, what's left of it, to a new master.

The months have taken their toll on her. Her face has grown haggard. Her eyes reflect the emptiness of the life she has been living. She is bent low, on her knees, with head bowed down—at the auction block, ready to be sold to the highest bidder.

Hosea, too, has come to the market, much as he had done so many years earlier. Again, his heart is heavy, not so much because of the sins of his people, but because of the tragedy of his wife. While making his purchase of fruit, he hears the bark of the auctioneer, "Who'll give two shekels? Do I hear three shekels or four?"

Hosea, sensing a strange pull, moves closer—perhaps to get a better look. And then, seeing, he cringes. He recognizes the bent wraith as Gomer. He turns away and then back again, somewhat dumbfounded, stunned, in shock. He listens as the offers are made. The bids are going nowhere. It's far too evident that Gomer's life has been spent.

The auctioneer is making his last call; the hammer is about to fall; the last bid, once, twice ... "Fifteen shekels," cries a voice from way in back. The townsfolk turn in the direction of the voice, and in amazement they find Hosea. They gawk and gape as this man of God makes his way forward and empties his purse before the auctioneer.

But Hosea isn't mindful of the townspeople. His eyes are fixed upon this woman, now wretched and desperate. He sees beyond her rags, her dirty skin and matted hair. He sees beyond the glassy, glazed look in her eyes. He only knows this is the love of his life, and he receives her. She is transformed in his mind's eye to that beautiful bride he met here long ago.

The time has come to take her home. He bends over her, enfolds her in his arms and lifts her up where she belongs. He takes her down off the auction block, out of the market, down the street to his home, their home.

The three children are there to meet them. Hosea calls them again by name, but things are different now. His first born, "Jezreel," will no longer refer to destruction but to a "bountiful harvest" which God will provide Israel. Their daughter, "Lo Ruhamah," ("no compassion") will be called "Ruhamah," or "compassion," for God will once again have compassion on his people. And "Lo Ami," ("not my people/son") will be called "Ami," or "my people, my son," for God will reclaim this wayward people for his own.

And what do Hosea and Gomer talk about that night? They pass over the intervening years, and he speaks tenderly to her, reminding her of her beauty, her charm and her grace.

Finally, come with me to the epilogue. We are now in the twentieth century, on the main street of your town. You and I are the characters in this true life story. We recognize ourselves in the role of Gomer. And Hosea's love reflects so splendidly the love which we have come to know from God.

Do we now have an idea of the incredible heartache we can bring to God by our actions and our attitudes? Can we imagine how it breaks his heart when we disregard his will? When we live on a lesser plain than he has for us? When we take his name in vain? When we mistreat others? When we live as though his Son had never died for us? Have we not all played the role of Gomer with God?

But God has made his way down to the main street of our lives, purchased us back, enfolded us in his arms, spoken tenderly to us and taken us home. He has acted toward us with compassion and called us his people, his children. He has restored us unto himself, demonstrating the matchless love of God.

Questions for Review

1. Did you sense some of the power of the Hebrew story? What are some of the unique strengths of this form?

2. Did you find yourself being drawn into the story, perhaps identifying with Hosea at some points—e.g., when he was called by God for a special task? When he first fell in love? When his heart was broken by the one he loved?

3. Did you identify with Hosea's wife, Gomer? And doesn't an understanding of the beauty of this name in the Hebrew help to redeem it from its unfortunate sound in English?

4. Can you think of times when you have broken the heart of God who loves you with an everlasting love?

5. Can you begin to comprehend the powerful, match-less love of God? Is it easier now for you to appreciate the lengths to which God has gone to bring you back to himself? Can you experience God's forgiveness and grace and feel washed, cleansed and renewed?

Three

Ruth Reclaims Divine Providence

The book of Ruth is one of the *megilloth*, or five "little books" (Ruth, Esther, Song of Songs, Lamentations and Ecclesiastes), which are read on feast days in the Jewish tradition. Each year the beautiful story of Ruth is read during the feast of *Shabuot*, or "Weeks," to celebrate the closing of the weeks of grain harvest. In such a context of the gleaning of grain, the story of Ruth the gleaner is especially appropriate.

Within classical literature the character of Ruth has been elevated to a lofty plain. In Bunyan's *Pilgrim's Progress* Ruth is the model for Christiana's companion, Mercy. For Milton she is the exemplary, virtuous lady. Keats and Goethe both laud her as well.

Interestingly enough, when we come to the Christian tradition, references to the magnificent story are strikingly lacking. Searching the Christian lectionaries (suggested biblical readings for worship) and worship resources for an allusion to Ruth will be in vain. It is a pity that we in the church have no directed occasion for the reading of this story which conveys so beautifully the quiet, sure working of God in the lives of his children.

The story begins by mentioning the name of a certain man of Bethlehem, Elimelech, which means, "God will rule." Take note of the name. Every name in Hebrew carries a meaning beyond itself, and this name is no exception. It is a name which conveys the underlying theme of this book: the rule of God.

Elimelech married Naomi and they had two sons. There was a famine in the land of Judah. The stalks of corn had dried and turned brown; the wheat and barley had been ruined. The entire land had grown weary from the drought. As Elimelech and his family looked across the Dead Sea to the plains of Moab, they observed the lush, green fields. They decided it was time for them to migrate to this fairer land.

But all was not well there. Soon, Elimelech, Naomi's husband, died. Their two sons took Moabite wives, Orpah and Ruth. But after ten years and no children the two sons died and Naomi was left a widow with little hope.

She determined that it was time to return to her own country; she had heard that there was again grain in Bethlehem. She would leave her two daughters-in-law, and so the three of them made their way to the river Jordan to say goodbye. As they prepare to part, the two daughters-in-law, Ruth and Orpah, raise objections, "We will go with you; we do not wish to part."

But Naomi insists, "There is no hope for you in my country. Return to your own people, and perhaps you will find hope among them."

Orpah obeys and turns back to Moab. But Ruth remains and utters those words which have since become immortal: "Don't urge me to leave you or to turn back from you. Where you go I will go, and where you stay I will stay. Your people will be my people and your God my God . . ." (Ruth 1:16).

Ruth returns with Naomi to Bethlehem. When they arrive the townspeople recognize them. They say, "Is this Naomi?" And she responds with bitterness, "Don't call me Naomi . . . [which in the Hebrew means 'fullness,' 'refreshment']; Call me Mara, [which in the Hebrew means 'bitterness'] because the Almighty has made my life very bitter" (Ruth 1:20). Thus the first chapter closes on this very low note.

But the second chapter opens by striking a note of hope. It begins this way: "Now Naomi had a relative on her husband's side . . . a man of standing, whose name was Boaz." Now if you know the ancient Levirite law, you know that the nearest of kin has an obligation to marry the woman who has been widowed (Deuteronomy 25:5-10). So we see an unmistakable spark of hope introduced.

In the ancient biblical world farmers left the outer fringes of their fields for the widows, orphans and the poor to glean. So Ruth goes out to glean, and it "just happens," as the storyteller states (you know how those providential circumstances "just happen"), that Ruth comes to the field which belongs to Boaz. And when it comes time to take the afternoon water break, Boaz notices her and asks his workers who she is. Then he promptly begins to make special provisions for her.

Curious about this, she asks, "Why are you doing this for me, a foreigner?"

"Because I have heard of your kindness to your mother-in-law, Naomi," is his reply.

Her reputation of caring has preceded her. And that evening when she eats her supper, she saves some food to take home to Naomi. It is a beautiful story of kindness and love.

Now it is Naomi's turn. She begins to plot a strategy for her daughter-in-law and Boaz. You know how mothers-in-law (and mothers) can be! She says, "Ruth, I suspect that Boaz is down at the threshing floor, threshing the grain. I think that you should take a nice warm bath, put on some of that aromatic perfume we have been saving, put on your best dress and drop by the threshing floor. But, oh yes, wait until after he has eaten and is satisfied."

Ruth obliges, "Everything you say I will do."

And indeed she does. Naomi's plan is going to be fulfilled, and soon all will be well, or so it seems. Ruth and Boaz fall in love, and just when it appears as though they are going to live happily ever after, Boaz remembers that there is someone who is a nearer next of kin than he. Suddenly it looks as though all is lost.

But behind the scenes (to the perceptive viewer) is the silent, subtle hand of God persistently at work. Boaz goes to the next of kin, explains the situation and works out a deal agreeable to both. Boaz marries Ruth, and they have a son named Obed, who later has a son named Jesse, who then has a son named David—that's right, King David, of the lineage of Jesus of Nazareth.

The story of Ruth conveys a threefold theological message: the magnetism of God's community, the kindness of God's people, the mystery of God's ways.

The Magnetism of God's Community

There is an attractiveness about God's people, a magnetism about God's community that draws other people. There is a quality of life that is appealing and captivating. God's community becomes a "contagious congregation," to employ the title of a book by George Hunter. Ruth was drawn to Naomi's religion because she was drawn to Naomi. And I suspect that is true of most of us. Was it a mother, father, friend or teacher who most influenced you in your walk with God? No doubt there was someone in whom you put your trust before you could put your trust in God. That is the genius of our Christian faith. The Word became flesh and dwelt among us. Only as the Word, the concept of God's love, becomes flesh again and again in the community of God's people will others be drawn to him.

There was a quality about Naomi that attracted Ruth

to Naomi, and not only to Naomi but also to Naomi's God, so that she proclaimed, "Thy God shall be my God." Will our children be able to make the same affirmation? Will our neighbors and friends?

A marvelous story comes to mind here, once related by the preeminent preacher of his day, J. Wallace Hamilton, entitled, "The Man With the Two Umbrellas." It is an episode from the life of Dr. Gordon Torgerson.

When he crossed the Atlantic one summer he noticed a dark-skinned man sitting in a deck chair and reading a Bible. One day he sat beside him and said, "Forgive my curiosity, but I'm a Baptist minister. I see you come here everyday and read your Bible. I assume you're a Christian, and I'm interested to know how it happened."

"Yes," said the man, setting aside his Bible, "I'm very happy to talk about it. I'm a Filipino. I was born in a good Catholic home in the Philippines, and some years ago I came to the United States to one of your fine universities to study law.

"My first night on campus, a student came to see me. He said, 'I've come over to welcome you to the campus and to say that if there is anything I can do to help make your stay more pleasant, I hope you'll call on me.' Then he asked me where I went to church, and I told him I was Catholic. He said, 'Well, I can tell you where the Catholic church is, but it's not easy to find; it's quite a distance away. Let me make a map.' So he made a map to the Catholic church and left.

"When I awakened Sunday morning it was raining. I thought to myself, I'll just forego church this morning; surely I can be forgiven for this. It's my first Sunday here, it's raining hard and the church is hard to find. I'll get some more sleep."

"Then there was a knock on the door, and when I opened it, there stood that student. His raincoat was dripping wet, and on one arm he had two umbrellas. He said, 'I thought you might have a hard time finding your church, especially in the rain, and I shall walk along with you and show you where it is.' As I got dressed, I thought, *What kind of fellow is this?* As we walked along in the rain under the two umbrellas, I said to myself, *if this fellow is so concerned about my religion, I ought to know something about his.* I asked, 'Where do you go to church?'

"'Oh,' he said, 'my church is just around the corner.'

"I said, 'Suppose we go to your church today and we'll go to my church next Sunday.' I went to his church, and I've never been back to my own. After four years, I felt I should change my career from law to ministry. I went to Drew Seminary, was ordained a Methodist minister and received an appointment to a Methodist church in the Philippines. My name is Valencius; I am Bishop Valencius, Bishop of the Methodist Church in the Philippines."[2]

The magnetism of God's community can still be a powerful force for the church.

The Kindness of God's People

Ruth's name in Hebrew means "friend" or "companion." She is the paradigm of extraordinary acts of kindness and loyalty. Surely it would have been more convenient for her to have stayed among her own people in Moab, but out of loyalty to Naomi she determined to be with her and look after her.

What is kindness? From the New Testament we learn that it is one of the fruit of the Spirit (Galatians 5:22). But if you ask an Old Testament writer what kindness is, he will tell you a story—the story of Ruth. She put her mother-in-law's welfare above her own. She gleaned in the field all day, and at dinner time she saved part of her meal for Naomi. Her kindness, done quietly, discreetly, became well known, so that Boaz heard of it even before he had met Ruth.

I remember years ago, as a teenager, hearing a story which I have never forgotten. An elderly woman walked into a J. C. Penney department store. Three young sales clerks were standing there (that was in the days when there were people around to wait on you), but her clothes were a bit tattered and worn, and they figured that it was a waste of their time to wait on such an unlikely prospect. But there was a fourth young man standing nearby, a devoted Christian for whom kindness was second nature. He approached the elderly woman, helped her make her purchases and then as she checked out, he learned that she was *Mrs. J. C. Penney.* An astute woman who knew exactly what had transpired, she made certain that this young man was quickly promoted—not simply as a reward for his kindness, but because she knew that anyone with that type of kindness would always have the best interests of the customer in mind.

The Mystery of God's Ways

In my view, the main point of the book of Ruth is to relate the sure, silent, mysterious workings of God on behalf of his children. The interpretations of the book of Ruth have gone through a substantial evolution. At first, it was viewed as simply a nice story, the relationship between Ruth and Boaz being depicted as a romantic tale. Then it was viewed as an example par excellence of loyalty and kindness. Currently in many circles, especially academic circles, the book of Ruth is regarded as an ecumenical tract, an attempt by the author to force the Jewish people beyond their narrow nationalism. The fact that the heroine is a foreigner and that she becomes the ancestress of King David supports this view.

There is merit to all three of these proposals, but they all fall short of the *theological* thrust of the story. I believe this little book is one of the most powerful theological statements in the Bible. It states so profoundly and portrays so effectively the truth that God's purposes are worked out in human affairs, often despite all appearances to the contrary. The theme of divine providence has seldom been conveyed so dramatically as in this simple story.

Did you notice the quiet, subtle ways God's hand is moving behind the scenes? God's purposes are barely visible. At times it appears as though they will not be accomplished, but they are! Do you recall the name of the first character in the story? It is Elimelech, which means, "God will rule." It is the providential rule of God that is portrayed so masterfully in this story of Ruth. First there is the famine, and that is bad news; yet there is hope because the family can go to the lush hills of Moab, and that is good news. But then Naomi's husband and her two sons die. She returns home a bitter woman ("Mara") because it appears that God has dealt bitterly with her. She is without hope.

I suspect that many of us have been at that point in our lives. It appears that God has dealt bitterly with us. God has turned against us. Life isn't worth living. But we learn from the book of Ruth that if we will but listen, the great Weaver of the tapestry of our lives is continuing to weave according to his purposes. And of course, a tapestry viewed from the back (or underside) is never clear. It often looks disjointed, as though some of the threads lead to dead ends. The irony is that you and I can never see the top side of the tapestry of our lives until after the fact.

Now just when the story of Ruth looks as if it is going to end on a note of bitterness, the second chapter reawakens hope. Ruth meets Boaz and they fall in love. At last God is going to bring good to Naomi and Ruth.

But wait, there is a complication: Boaz is not the closest kinsman. Someone else has the right and obligation to marry Ruth. Again we are plunged into questioning and despair. What is to become of Ruth and Naomi? The fourth chapter opens with Boaz enacting his plan. He gains the right to marry Ruth, they have a child and the purposes of God are accomplished.

In these four chapters we have a marvelous portrayal of the quiet, sure moving of the hand of almighty God. The author is saying, "God hears our prayers; God is moving behind the scenes; 'he who watches over Israel will neither slumber nor sleep'" (Psalm 121:4).

If God will take a young Moabite girl and direct her

paths, surely he will direct yours. Your life may have come to a standstill; your marriage may appear to be moving toward ruin; problems at work may seem overwhelming; but there is a woman named Ruth who can attest to the incredible faithfulness of God.

Questions for Review

1. Were you able to see how this is much more than just a "kind little story"? Did you perceive the theological theme of divine providence as the story unfolded and turned on seemingly insignificant events? Can you perceive the same divine providence operating in your life? And when you cannot *perceive* it, can you *believe* it, on the basis of this story?

2. Is there a magnetism about your congregation that draws people to church and to God? What are some ways you can develop that magnetism more fully?

3. Kindness is one aspect of the fruit of the Spirit. Like all fruit, it takes time and nurture. How can you become a kinder person?

4. Ruth was not one of the "people of God"; that is, she was not a Hebrew but rather belonged to the Moabite people, who were often regarded as bitter enemies of Israel. And yet God's providential plans included her. Is it possible for one's nationalism to be too restrictive, and thereby closed to the fact that God works among all peoples? Reflect on this in your life.

Four

Esther
Recognizes
Responsibility

The book of Esther is another of the *megilloth*, or five "little books" which are read on feast days in the Jewish tradition. This intriguing and enthralling story of Queen Esther is read during the festival of *Purim* in mid-March to celebrate God's victory over the enemies of the Jewish people. Perhaps you have seen children wearing costumes similar to those worn on Halloween; these Jewish children were celebrating *Purim*.

It is worth noting that when the religious leaders were deciding which books should be included as part of the Bible, or Canon, there was strong objection to the inclusion of the book of Esther. Indeed, several reasons support this objection: the book makes no mention of God, it contains little of ethical value, and there seems to be an unfortunate relishing of the punishment of non-Jews. Nevertheless, I believe there is a strong and significant message from God for us in this sacred book. Let's look at the story together.

In the year 470 B.C., Ahasuerus was king over Persia.

His rule extended over most of the known world. If the name Ahasuerus is unfamiliar to you, it should be; this is a rather unusual name given to Xerxes.

On a special occasion, Ahasuerus gave a grand and eloquent banquet for all his people, a truly lavish affair that lasted 180 days. It would have made the Mardi Gras seem insignificant. Partway through the feast, Ahasuerus decided it was time to show off Queen Vashti, for she was exceptionally beautiful. So he ordered an attendant to bring Queen Vashti before the crowds. The problem, however, was that she was tired of being put on display and paraded before the people, so she refused.

Kings are not accustomed to having their requests denied, and King Ahasuerus was no exception. He became enraged. He called together his counselors and asked their advice on this very serious matter. What should be done?

One self-serving soul spoke up, "Now listen, O King, Queen Vashti has not only wronged you, but every man in the kingdom has been wronged by her as well. Once word gets out, as it surely will, that she has disobeyed her husband the king, every woman in the realm will follow suit. No man alive is going to be given the respect and obedience he deserves if Queen Vashti gets away with this. You must do something immediately, O King."

Let me interject here a word about women's rights. It seems clear to me that the view of King Ahasuerus, that women are to be obedient subordinates, is antiquarian and unbiblical. The idea that women are to subject themselves passively to men is contrary to the Old Testament doctrine of creation, that we are all created in the image of God and bear God's mark on our lives. It runs counter to the New Testament teaching that in Christ we are all one. And it is simply wrong to think of one as superior over the other. Equal rights is a divine "given." Paul was divinely inspired in the book of Ephesians when he wrote of *mutual subjection* in the marriage relationship, being subject to one another, as unto Christ (Ephesians 5:21). This is the Christian way.

Back to the story of Esther. The king banished Vashti from the throne, and immediately a search went out across the entire realm in an effort to find the most beautiful young woman in the kingdom. They found Esther (sometimes called Hadassah), an orphan girl who had been adopted by her uncle, Mordecai. When she came before the king, as the scripture reads, "the king was attracted to Esther more than to any of the other women, and she won his favor and approval more than any of the other virgins. So he set a royal crown on her head and made her queen instead of Vashti" (2:17).

Enter the villain, Haman. He held a high position in the Persian government—so high, in fact, that whenever he passed by, all the people bowed down before him. All bowed except Mordecai, because as a Jew, one of the people of God, he would bow down only before God.

To be sure, this did not sit well with Haman, and he began to plot to destroy Mordecai and all the Jews with him (clearly, anti-Semitism is not just a recent travesty). So he convinced the king that the Jews were unpatriotic and subversive, and ought to be destroyed. Immediately a letter was issued across the realm with instructions to destroy, slay and annihilate all the Jews, young and old, women and children on one day, the thirteenth of March.

When Mordecai learned of this, he was mortified and sent word to Esther to go before the king and ask him to change the decree. But she sent back this word, "Everyone knows that if you go before the king without being called you will be put to death, and I am afraid that is what will happen to me, unless I find favor in his sight."

But Mordecai was not impressed. He replied, "Now listen, Esther. All your people need you. *Who knows but that for such a time as this you have come into the kingdom.*"

"All right," she said, "but you and my people need to fast and pray for three days before I try this."

After three days Esther came before the king in fear and trembling, but found favor in his sight. He said in effect, "Your wish is my command; ask whatever you want and I will grant it."

Instead of making her request, she invited the king and Haman to a banquet in their honor. So the king called Haman, the villain, unsuspecting soul that he was, and they went to the banquet. Again he asked, "Your wish is my command. What is your request, Queen Esther, and I will grant it?"

"I would like for you to come again tomorrow for dinner and then I will tell you my request," she replied.

So they came the next night. Haman was very excited to be such a valued guest. After dinner, the king asked the queen yet another time for her request.

She replied, "O King, someone has plotted against me and my people to destroy us."

The king arose in anger, "Who has planned such a terrible deed?" he demanded.

Esther, pointing to Haman, replied, "This wicked Haman!"

Immediately Haman was taken out and hanged from the gallows. And so Haman was destroyed and the Jews were rescued, and the holiday is celebrated each year in mid-March; it is the festival of *Purim*.

Now, what might be God's word for us from this book of Esther? I believe it is found primarily in 4:14 "And who knows whether you have not come to the kingdom for such a time as this?" (RSV).

In the previous chapter we looked at the book of Ruth, and noted that the main point of the book was the affirmation of the mysterious, silent, sure moving of the hand of God in human affairs. God was the chief actor. It was God who was working in all the circumstances of the lives of Naomi, Ruth and Boaz to accomplish his purposes.

A large portion of the Bible is about the *activity of God*. Divine activity is the primary theme of the Bible. But the book of Esther focuses on a different aspect—not a contradictory one, but a complimentary one: *human activity*.

Divine activity—human activity, God's power—human responsibility are two interrelated and delicately balanced phenomena.

The miracles of the Bible and of our own experiences are vital. Prayer is essential. Trust in God is crucial. All of these attest to the supernatural activity of God. These we affirm; we have experienced them and look for them with joy. But there are times when human beings need to step forward themselves and be responsible. Esther could have said, "Oh, let's ask God for a miracle," or "Let's just pray for a resolution," or "Let's just trust in God." Instead, Mordecai insisted, "But *you* have come to the kingdom for such a time as this! God will do his part, but *you* have been placed here for this particular crisis, and *you* must stand up and be counted!"

You see, in the divine scheme of things, in the world of the Bible and indeed in our world, these two elements, the divine and the human, are always interrelated. They work together like a finely tuned engine, like the proper meshing of two gears, like balanced weights on a set of scales. But in the history of the church, people have tended to err on one side or the other. The liberal folk tend to err on the side of emphasizing solely the *human*. According to their viewpoint God is just an idea, and does not come into play in our lives. If human society is going to be transformed, they say, it will be because *human beings* do it. "Don't look to the divine," "don't count on prayer," "there are no such things as miracles," or so they argue.

But this is certainly wrong. Without divine intervention, without the presence, power and blessing of almighty God, then whatever you and I do is inadequate. I have spoken with lots of folks who say, "I was trying my absolute best, but without prayer, and without the power of God, I could not have done it." And they are correct. We need to pray, we need to trust, we need to depend upon the "wonder-working power of God."

But there is also the tendency to err on the other side, to emphasize *only* the divine. This mistaken and misguided view holds that God does everything; we do nothing.

We expect God to perform a miracle—when *we* ought to be doing something.

We want God to straighten out our marriages—when *we* ought to start understanding and affirming our mates.

We want God to make sense out of our kids—when *we* ought to be trying to understand them.

We want God to take care of the poor when *we* ought to extend a helping hand.

Such a view pleads for total divine responsibility and no human accountability. But that is not the biblical way. We must remember the biblical record.

God *did* part the Red Sea, but if the children of Israel had not run through the waters, they would never have been set free.

God *did* deliver Goliath to David, but David had to step forward in battle and sling the stones at the giant.

God *does* save and redeem us miraculously, but Jesus had to climb on that cross to die in our place.

All of life is characterized by this divine/human co-operation. Because for such a time as this, God calls forth his people, and together, in dependency, in trust, the will of God is accomplished. Someone said it well, "We should pray as if everything depends on God and work as if everything depends on us."

That is why we affirm the very best in psychology, in medicine and in human understanding and skill; that is the human side, our responsibility. But we also affirm miracles, divine healings, prayer—that's the divine. Divine/human cooperation, that is the biblical way, the way that accords with reality.

The text reads, ". . . for such a time as this. . . ." Let's pursue it further—when is "this" time? It could be anytime, could it not?

"For such a time as this" could refer to our family relationships. "This" is a time in which we should pray fervently for our children and our marriages, but, in addition, we must step forward and *do* something.

I have a friend who never gave his family a compliment. A close friend confronted him on it once, and the man replied, "My wife and kids should assume that I like what they are doing unless I correct them." That is a *terrible* way to raise a family. Affirmation and encouragement are as vital to a healthy family as are the vitamins in our food.

A painful memory comes back to haunt me, even so many years after the fact. My father, my five brothers and I had just come in from making hay on our farm in Ohio. We were eagerly enjoying one of my mother's delicious dinners. Earlier that day Mom had gone to town and purchased a new dress, a fairly rare occurrence for a farm wife. During the meal she got up to put the new dress on and model it for her family. She came into the kitchen and did a partial twirl. We barely took the time to lift our heads from stuffing our faces to acknowledge her presence. I can still see her leaving the kitchen, holding back tears. We were a religious family, but "for such a time as this" we had failed to affirm and appreciate our mother.

Or let me ask you about your children. A sensitive parent from my congregation shared the following poem with me. It captures so powerfully the importance of human affirmation in our families. Make no mistake about it, it carries a powerful theological message and is entitled simply, "Words."

Today I said, "Clean your room right now."
I failed to say, "Thanks for doing a neat job."
Today I said, "You're late. Hurry up!"
I failed to say, "I enjoy having you around."
Today I said, "How in the world did you tear your jeans?"
I failed to say, "You're more important than things to me."

Today I said, "Look at this mess!"
I failed to say, "I like the way you share with friends."
Today I said, "Don't talk so loud.'
I failed to say, "Your ideas are important to me."
Today I said, "Don't forget to empty the trash."
I failed to say, "You accept responsibility well."
Today I said, "I wish you'd stop that silly giggling."
I failed to say, "I'm glad you're so happy today."
Today I said, "Have you finished your homework?"
I failed to say, "I'm glad you do your best."
Today I said, "I'm too busy."
I failed to say, "Let's do something together."
Today I said, "I need some peace and quiet."
I failed to say, "I'm glad you're my child."
Today I said, "Don't ever do that again."
I failed to say, "I love you."
Father, may my corrections and complaints never outweigh my expressions of love. Guide my tongue to express encouragement, acceptance, and love to my children every day. Amen. [3]

" . . . for such a time as this. . . . " What is the "this"? Perhaps we could apply this principle to our own personal struggle. Here is a great "mystery," to use Pauline terminology: it is in the *human doing* that we attain our highest potential. It was true of Esther; it will be true of us. There are some folk who think that God should have prevented us from having to struggle; he should have left out of our lives the agonies, difficulties, struggles and stresses. Life should have been all ease and leisure. But the fact is that God can never make great people without great tasks. To be sure, much popular religion of our day would like to avoid this reality by escaping to a fairy tale land in which God is on hand to meet our every need. But that would cheapen us. It would weaken us.

God continues to call us for "such a time as this." He will not do for us what we can and should do for ourselves. And it is in our human responding that we become all that we are created to be.

44

Questions for Review

1. The books of Ruth and Esther present two parts of the larger picture of God's truth. The former focuses on God's providence, while the latter is concerned more with human responsibility. Do you tend to emphasize one over the other in your own view of life? Which one? Why? What might you do to achieve a greater balance?

2. Could you feel Esther's anxiety about following her uncle's instructions? The *right* thing is often not the easy thing. Is there something you know you should do, but you have been hesitating, maybe even praying that God would "deliver" you from having to do it? What are you going to do?

3. If you are a parent, then God has called you to that task for this time. How effective are you in affirming your child's self-esteem? Have you read any good books about parenting? Are you relying too heavily on the philosophy of "whatever will be, will be"? Are you expecting God simply to take care of things? Or are you taking up your own responsibility?

4. Is there a moral issue in your community that will be addressed only if you and your congregation address it?

5. It is intriguing how God's will is almost always enacted through human responsibility, isn't it? Consider any application in your own life.

Five

Ecclesiastes Reassures Our Doubts

He questioned everything. Always analyzing, ever doubting. He wouldn't accept anything at face value. A modern day doubting Thomas, that's how his friends described him.

The "him" in this case was me. Perhaps that is why I have been drawn to the most unusual and remarkable portion of the Old Testament—the book of Ecclesiastes, sometimes known as *Koheleth*, Hebrew for "the preacher."

Some have called Ecclesiastes "the most dangerous book in the Bible" because it challenges nearly every idea that the rest of the Bible holds sacred. It was considered so dangerous that many rabbis wanted to ban it, lest young innocent readers find it and be corrupted by it. Indeed, it was highly questionable whether the book of Ecclesiastes would be included in the Canon at all.

It begins on a depressing note and goes downhill from there. "Vanity of vanities, says the Preacher, vanity of vanities! All is vanity," (Ecclesiastes 1:2, RSV) is the opening line, right after the heading. This is followed by a remarkable litany of fatalism, which is otherwise so foreign to the Bible.

1. There is no point in working, for what does a person gain for all his or her efforts (v. 3)?
2. People come and people go and nothing ever changes (v. 4).
3. Everything has been set in motion and nothing will ever change. The sun rises and sets; the winds blow and the streams flow in predetermined fashion (vv. 5-7).
4. There is nothing new under the sun (vv. 9-11).
5. Any honest investigation will show that God has afflicted us with an unhappy lot (vv. 12-14).
6. We are locked in the grip of fatalism: What is twisted cannot be straightened; what is lacking cannot be counted (v. 15).
7. Life itself is pointless—it is simply a striving after wind (v. 17).
8. What's more, if you increase your knowledge, you only increase your sorrow (v. 18).

That is the introductory chapter to the book of Ecclesiastes! It is a depressing picture, but it gets worse. Some of the most valued truths of the Old Testament continue to be rigorously challenged and discarded.

1. What about the time-tested distinction between the wise person and the fool that runs throughout the book of Proverbs? Forget it, because they each have the same fate: " . . . the wise man dies just like the fool!" (2:16, RSV).
2. What about the value and dignity of work stated so eloquently in the creation story? Koheleth, the preacher, rejects it. All his labor was for naught, "So I . . . gave my heart up to despair over all the toil of my labors under the sun . . . This also is vanity and great evil" (2:18-23, RSV).
3. What about the high purpose and meaning in life that was an integral part of the Hebrew tradition? He discards this notion and adopts the Epicurean philosophy of "Eat, drink and be merry," an idea unheard of in the rest of the Old Testament (2:24; see also 5:18; 8:15).

48

4. And what of the sanctity of human life, a clarion trademark in the Judeo-Christian faith? It too is disparaged, "Man's fate is like the that of the animals; the same fate awaits them both: As one dies, so dies the other. . . . Everything is meaningless. All go to the same place; all come from dust, and to dust all return" (3:19, 20). The dead are better off than the living, and better yet are they who will not be born (4:1-3).

Why then was this book ever permitted to become part of the sacred Scriptures? Of course no one knows for sure, but in my view, its mere inclusion in the Bible is bold recognition of the fact that all of us have our times of skepticism and doubt. Who has never wondered if there really is any purpose in life? Who, in moments of honest reflection, has not felt himself or herself locked in the grip of fatalistic forces?

I deeply appreciate the book of Ecclesiastes because I, too, have been in the valley of despair and have questioned everything under the sun. It is good to know that God does not disparage such honest doubt, but rather encourages it, as witnessed by the fact that this remarkable book is a part of God's sacred Word.

I well remember the day that I stood beside the grave of a young man who had committed suicide. I tried to communicate care and concern. I spoke of God's love and grace. I spoke of our resurrection hope. But the thought came pounding into my head and heart relentlessly, "Isn't this really all there is—this hole, the dirt and dust?" I am both ashamed and amazed at this question that arose from within my heart. Then I open the Bible and, in the midst of God's sacred words of promise, I find the word of another preacher who questions and doubts more deeply than I the meaning of life itself.

I do not want to dwell in this book very long, nor do I wish to read it exclusively. But I am grateful that I can stop by for awhile and listen to one who gives eloquent expression to the feelings of doubt, despair and futility that I have known from time to time.

Ecclesiastes is a reminder that the Bible is not a monolithic composition, but is as diverse as we are. The Word of God is replete with crashing cymbals of thanksgiving, unmatched songs of praise and triumphant hymns of joy. It is blessed with an abundance of stories of heroes of the faith: Sarah and Abraham, Deborah, Gideon, Ruth, Mary, Peter and John. There is more than enough material here to inspire and challenge the best of us.

But the force of its diversity comes through in places like the utter honesty of the story of David and Nathan after David's adulterous affair with Bathsheba (no other ancient historical document would have included such an indicting story of the king). We see the diversity also in the psalms of lament, which pick up the anguished cry of the bereaved, the oppressed and the distraught. All of life is not joyous; indeed there is much to lament, and nowhere in all of literature is expression given to this aspect of life like it is in more than half of the Psalms, the psalms of lament. Ecclesiastes stands with these documents of diversity, touching a nerve with everyone who has ever wondered honestly about the underside of life.

Now, there are some who have moved easily into the faith and have never doubted once through their years as believers. They have never questioned, have never been skeptical about God and the life of faith. My wife is such a person—a person of deep faith and prayer. She and those like her are fortunate indeed, and the Christian community is greatly enriched by their ministry of prayer and faith.

But there are a host of us who at one time or another have found ourselves overwhelmed by dark doubts, penetrating questions and debilitating skepticism. The book of Ecclesiastes is for folks like us.

It seems that there are seasons in our lives, times when doubts affect us more than they do at other times. I think the preacher, Koheleth, knew of this movement of the seasons, for after all, he penned those immortal lines:

> There is a time for everything, and a season
> for every activity under heaven:
> a time to be born and a time to die,
> a time to plant and a time to uproot,
> a time to kill and a time to heal,
> a time to tear down and a time to build,
> a time to weep and a time to laugh,
> a time to mourn and a time to dance,
> a time to scatter stones and a time to gather them,
> a time to embrace and a time to refrain,
> a time to search and a time to give up,
> a time to keep and a time to throw away,
> a time to tear and a time to mend,
> a time to be silent and a time to speak,
> a time to love and a time to hate,
> a time for war and a time for peace (3:1-8).

Do you suppose that Koheleth could be so honest with his times of doubt and despair because he had learned that they were simply part of the seasons of life? There *is* a time for questioning and a time for believing; a time for skepticism and a time for faith. For most of us, it is a part of the ebb and flow of life. So do not be surprised when those times come—ride them through.

I think that for most of us, there are two major seasons of doubt. The first is adolescence. In the early stage, young people doubt themselves. Insecurities abound. The approval of their friends is of preeminent importance. Later on, high school and college students question everything. They doubt all traditions and wonder if their parents have any sense at all. It is part of the seasonal flow. And the trick for parents, says James Dobson, is simply to survive. Ride the wave, believing that it will eventually level out. Do not do anything disastrous. It is the season, and this season, like all seasons, will yield to the next one.

Too often parents become offended at the thinking of their kids. They forbid them from thinking such things. You cannot prevent it; it is the season. This is a normal part of the process of breaking free, of becoming independent, self-reliant adults, which any healthy parent wants for his or her child.

But I have two words for young persons who are going through this. First, *recognize that these periods of questioning are normal and healthy.* You are doing what every generation has done before you. It is God's way of allowing you to develop a mind of your own.

Second, *learn that some day you will need to work through your skeptical moods.* As Harry Emerson Fosdick put it, you must learn to "doubt your doubts." Doubts and questions always eventually lead to affirmations. You cannot for long build your life on what you *don't* believe. Somewhere down the road you need to establish what you *do* believe.

The second major season is that of mid-life, home of the "mid-life crisis." Look for it; it is going to come in one form or another. It was probably at this age that the author of Ecclesiastes wrote. He looked around at all he had done, and all he could say was, "Vanity of vanities, all is vanity. What is the point of it all?"

Rabbi Harold Kushner, the author who was made famous through his book, *When Bad Things Happen to Good People*, has written another book entitled, *When All You've Ever Wanted Isn't Enough.* It is based on Ecclesiastes. He makes the point that when you come to the place in your life, as the preacher did, when you first realize that everything you have attained isn't enough, it is devastating. But it can become a time of opportunity to move on to genuine faith and authentic living.

Paul Tsongas, successful political figure from Massachusetts, was very much on track to run for President of the United States. While taking a shower one morning, he discovered a lump under his skin. Investigation showed that it was cancerous. All of life began to take on a new meaning. Suddenly it wasn't so important to be in Washington every free moment. Time at home with his wife and three daughters became his main priority. He had come to the point where all he had ever wanted in life wasn't enough. And at that point he began to discover what really mattered.

As I write these words, I am at a retreat center in central Florida. The main speaker is Peter Storey, prominent churchman from South Africa, who has been a leading witness against apartheid during his thirty years of ministry. In the process of racially integrating his congregation, he received more than two hundred letters of withdrawal. They came slowly, over a period of time. Each one, he said, was like a knife piercing his side. His words still ring in my ears: "Living through the fires of apartheid has a way of burning away everything that is extra, and leaving only that which is real." You can see that *reality* in his life.

Maybe, just maybe, the season of doubt that God allows into our lives is intended to be just such a time of purging away the dross and leaving us with what really matters.

And what is really of consequence? Koheleth comes to it at the end of his long season of skepticism and doubt. At the end of the book he arrives at "the end of the matter" (12:13, RSV), i.e., that which is truly important. It is this: give reverence to God and obey his commandments.

I am reminded of a conversation with a friend whom I was visiting in Cambridge, England. He is a brilliant scholar in New Testament studies, a profound thinker and genuine person. We were talking about the complexities of life in general and the Christian life in particular.

"What is the rock bottom essence of the Christian life?" I asked. "I think I have found it," he said. "It sounds much too simple, but I am convinced of its merit. It is found in the old song whose chorus goes like this: 'Trust and obey, for there's no other way to be happy in Jesus, but to trust and obey.'"

Some people come to this accurate assessment easily; others of us must take the circuitous route that runs through the book of Ecclesiastes.

Questions for Review

1. Are you one of those for whom faith has come easily, or are you one who has had to come through the twisting and turbulent avenues of doubt and skepticism? Why do you think that is so?

2. Describe your journey of faith. There is no right and wrong way to come to faith, but it is helpful to understand the route that we each took. It is also important not to prescribe that same route for everyone else.

3. Are you pleased or displeased that a book like Ecclesiastes is in the Bible? Why?

4. How did you approach (or how are you approaching) the various seasons of life? Were/are you prepared? Does it make sense that realizing there are natural seasons to life should make them less traumatic?

5. Are you allowing your children to experience their own season of doubt? It may be a necessary prelude to faith. Reflect on why it is often so difficult for conscientious parents to allow their children to go through the season of adolescence. What resources have you found helpful in weathering these storms?

Six

The Song of Songs Reveres Love

We come now to what is arguably the greatest love song ever written. Indeed, its lofty status is suggested by its title, *The Song of Songs*, i.e., the greatest of all songs (compare the title for Jesus as the "King of Kings" which implies that he is "the greatest of all kings"). You may know it as *The Song of Solomon*, but it is exegetically clear from the opening Hebrew words, *shir hashirim*, that the proper name is *The Song of Songs*. Certainly it is among the most exquisite and beautiful of all love songs.

Even a cursory reading of this short book reveals a language that is both explicit and graphic. We are caught unaware, as it were, by the clear and even suggestive references to the human body. This has proven problematic to interpreters throughout the centuries. Many of them simply could not believe that a sacred book of Scripture would refer so openly to human sexual love. Therefore these interpreters insisted that this beautiful song must be interpreted solely allegorically. That is to say, the depic-

55

tion of the love between a man and a woman must be *elevated* to refer to the relationship between God and Israel (Jewish interpreters) or Christ and the church (Christian commentators). Or, in a slight variation of this approach, the song was interpreted to support the Roman Catholic notion of Mariology, which saw the blessed virgin Mary as the bride of Christ in the Song of Songs.

I have come to believe, with many present day commentators, that the sacred song has at least two levels of meaning. The allegorical interpretation is one, but it is secondary. The primary interpretation—the one that was intended by the author—is the literal interpretation. This sacred song is to be seen first and foremost as the celebration of human sexual love and the unbounded pleasure that a man and woman can experience in sexual union. In that it is a marvelous, wonderful portion of Scripture.

There is no reason why biblical interpreters or Christians of any sort should feel uncomfortable with this interpretation. God made woman and man in his own image and said that it is "very good" (Genesis 1:31). Then he gave them to each other to enjoy and commanded them to become one flesh. The Bible says, "the man and his wife were both naked and *they felt no shame*" (Genesis 2:25). And, because God's word touches on the whole gamut of human relationships, it is especially appropriate that there be an entire book written in melodic fashion to celebrate the joys of human sexual love.

A book like the Song of Songs is always timely, but perhaps even more so today. We are bombarded more than ever before with so many unhealthy notions of sex. From the soaps in the afternoon to "Golden Girls" on Saturday night, sex is portrayed as either a tool for manipulation or a subject for silly jokes. Lonely men and women sit glued to their television sets each afternoon hoping for some vicarious satisfaction, and on Saturday nights they enjoy an empty laugh that mocks, if not disguises, the lack of joy and pleasure in their own relationships.

SONG OF SONGS

I think of our young people, bright, talented, full of life
and promise. They have experienced within their bodies
all of the wonderfully mysterious changes that come with
their age and which draw them toward the opposite sex.
They fall in love but aren't sure what that means or how
to express it. And often the only models of sexual expression come from all the wrong places.

It is little wonder that in this sex-saturated society we
know so little of sexual satisfaction. It seems that the more
our culture talks about sex, the less we enjoy it; the more
sex is portrayed on the movie screen, the less we delight in
it at home.

What has been the church's voice in all of this? Primarily it has been one of opposition. An edition of the *American
Family Association Journal* (October, 1988) strikes a
clarion call against indecency. Note these telling headlines:
"Assemblies of God Group Joins Holiday Inn Boycott" (for
its in-room pornographic movies); "Morality in Media Has
'White Ribbon' Campaign—White Ribbon Against Pornog-
raphy (WRAP)"; "What Can Citizens Do About Obscene
Videos Rented in Local Stores?" Everyone knows what we
are against, but for heaven's sake, what are we *for*?

How is it possible that a church which has recorded
within its sacred writings a book like Song of Songs appears unable to make a positive statement about the
beauty, joy and pleasure of sexual love? Have you ever read
a more wonderful expression of a man's appreciation for
his wife and the beauty of her body than this one, from
Song of Songs?

How beautiful you are, my darling!
Oh, how beautiful!
Your eyes behind your veil are doves.
Your hair is like a flock of goats
descending from Mount Gilead.
Your teeth are like a flock of sheep just shorn,
coming up from the washing.
Each has its twin;
not one of them is alone.

57

Your lips are like a scarlet ribbon;
your mouth is lovely.
Your temples behind your veil
are like the halves of a pomegranate.
Your neck is like the tower of David,
built with elegance;
on it hang a thousand shields,
all of them shields of warriors.
Your two breasts are like two fawns,
like twin fawns of a gazelle
that browse among the lilies (4:1-5).

Or a wife's appreciation for her husband:

My lover is radiant and ruddy,
outstanding among ten thousand.
His head is purest gold;
his hair is wavy and black as a raven.
His eyes are like doves
by the water streams,
washed in milk, mounted like jewels.
His cheeks are like beds of spice
yielding perfume.
His lips are like lilies dripping with myrrh.
His arms are rods of gold set with chrysolite.
His body is like polished ivory decorated with sapphires.
His legs are pillars of marble
set on bases of pure gold.
His appearance is like Lebanon,
choice as its cedars.
His mouth is sweetness itself;
he is altogether lovely.
This is my lover, this my friend,
O daughters of Jerusalem (5:10-16).

Many in the ancient world thought of the body as evil; therefore, such a celebration as we find in this sacred song would have been unthinkable. There were a number of Greeks who held this negative view of the body. Their philosophy was called docetism, which held that only the spirit was good; matter was considered evil. Therefore the flesh was evil, and because the flesh was so evil there was

58

no way that Jesus, the Son of God, could have taken bodily form. They said that was really an illusion; Jesus was only spirit. This philosophy was in vogue when John wrote his gospel. How powerful, then, his opening words, "In the beginning was the Word (Jesus). . . . The Word became flesh and made his dwelling among us" (John 1:1, 14a). The elevation of the physical could not have been more pronounced.

For the Buddhists, the human body is viewed as restrictive, a hindrance to genuine spiritual development. The chief goal of life is to move out of this bodily state to a state of non-existence called nirvana. To that end, Buddha proposed his famous eight-fold path.

Or take the peoples all around ancient Israel. They held a low regard for the human body. Therefore, it was commonplace to see unclothed statues of men and women. But the Hebrews had a different idea: The body, created by God in his own image, is sacred, so sacred that it ought to be covered, to be revealed only to one other person in marital sexual union.

This notion of covering is intriguing. I find it interesting that in ancient Israel's worship, one moved ever inward from the outer temple (which was fully exposed) to the inner temple, and one moved still further to that sacred place, the Holy of Holies, which is covered, shrouded in mystery. The human body, particularly those life-yielding parts, because of their mystery, were to be covered so that they may be uncovered and fully shared in the mysterious union of marital sexual love.

This connection between the religious and the sexual is particularly interesting. In the Hebrew language the same word is used for both—one's relationship with God and one's sexual relationship with a spouse. The word is *ydh*, and it means "to know." "Now Adam *knew* Eve his wife and she conceived and bore Cain . . . " (Genesis 4:1, RSV). Then in John's gospel we read, "Now this is eternal life: that they may *know* you, the only true God, and Jesus

Christ, whom you have sent" (John 17:3). In both instances the focus is on an intimate, personal relationship. Dare I suggest that I doubt whether one can fully know another human being unless and until one knows God in an intimate way?

I shall never forget my first pastoral assignment. I was the assistant pastor, primarily a youth director. I had inherited an extremely sharp youth group. They were kids who had just made vital commitments to Jesus Christ. They were eager to study the Bible. Their thirst for God's Word and God's ways was exhilarating.

But they lived by the ocean and were very much influenced by their friends and the local culture. They wore hardly any clothes! And the clothes they wore were terribly revealing. After one of the Bible studies I said to them, "You know, God loves you so much and wants you to be able to share yourself fully and intimately with someone very special down the road. In the meantime you need to protect those beautiful parts of your bodies. Cover them and keep them for that one special person, so that one day you and your beloved will enjoy them beyond words."

Those kids took that to heart. "Interestingly enough, it was a turning point. It was a *kairos* moment for them, a time of transformation. It seemed that until this very intimate part of their lives was brought into focus, the other intimate side, the spiritual, could not develop fully. Today, when I see many of those kids now grown up and having meaningful ministries with other young people, they refer back to that night after the Bible study as a decisive turning point in their lives.

We receive *Sports Illustrated* at our house, or more exactly, our son Darin does. He loves sports and his grandparents sent him a subscription. Not long ago, the annual swimsuit edition arrived, and my wife Jan intercepted it before Darin came home from school. When I came home, and the kids were outside, Jan pulled out the magazine and asked, "What are we going to do with this?"

I considered those revealing swimsuits and replied, "We can talk through it with Darin now, or we can wait awhile. He is only in the fifth grade. Let's wait if we can."

Well, a few days later, around the dinner table, Darin announced, "Those guys from *Sports Illustrated* didn't send me this week's copy, so I called them and they said they would put one in the mail today."

It was clear that the time had come to discuss it, so while Darin and I were playing basketball I asked him to bring me the magazine lying on his mother's desk. A few seconds later he came out with the "missing" copy.

"Darin, this is pretty strong stuff," I said. "Do you mind if we look through it together? These pictures are pretty revealing, aren't they? And it is absolutely normal for any healthy boy to enjoy looking at them. But there are two problems: First, they uncover parts of each woman that should be covered and kept only for the man with whom she will spend the rest of her life. Second, pictures are only an imitation of the real thing, and the real thing is so wonderful that we want to wait until the right time to enjoy it fully. Your mother and I believe the right time is when two people are married."

The ensuing discussion was one of the most precious times of sharing we have ever experienced, and interestingly enough, Darin felt greatly affirmed by our conversation. I feel in my heart of hearts that God placed his blessings on our time together.

A few years ago *Redbook* magazine conducted an extensive survey of its readers. They were exploring the aspects of sexual practices and sexual enjoyment. Several thousand responses were returned. The editors were shocked at what the survey revealed. In a nutshell it was this: Religious women have more fun. They, the survey suggested, were the ones who had the greatest emotional and sexual satisfaction.

It was a surprise to the editors; it would not have been a surprise to the author of Song of Songs. In the security of their faith commitments and the sanctity of their marriages, these women could enjoy all the pleasures of sex without inhibition or guilt.

It has been my conviction that there are many treasures in the Old Testament. And both the church and the world are the poorer for their neglect. Perhaps the area where this neglect strikes home most intimately is in our hesitation to proclaim the beauty, the joy, the pleasure and the ecstasy of marital sexual love. Wouldn't it be wonderful if the church could help couples to:

• Recapture the sense of anticipation revealed in these words:
> Listen! My lover!
> Look! Here he comes,
> leaping across the mountains,
> bounding over the hills (2:8).

• Rediscover the tenderness of:
> He has taken me to the banquet hall,
> and his banner over me is love (2:4).

• Renew the sense of joyous commitment:
> My lover is mine and I am his (2:16).

• Rekindle the romance of:
> You have stolen my heart, my sister, my bride;
> you have stolen my heart with one glance of your eyes,
> with one jewel of your necklace.
> How delightful is your love, my sister, my bride!
> How much more pleasing is your love than wine,
> and the fragrance of your perfume than any spice!
> Awake, north wind, and come, south wind!
> Blow on my garden,
> that its fragrance may spread abroad.
> Let my lover come into his garden
> and taste its choice fruits (4:9-10, 16).

•Reawaken sexual pleasure:
> How beautiful you are and how pleasing,

Oh love, with your delights!
Your stature is like that of the palm,
and your breasts like clusters of fruit.
I said, "I will climb the palm tree;
I will take hold of its fruit."
May your breasts be like the clusters of the vine,
the fragrance of your breath like apples,
and your mouth like the best wine.
May the wine go straight to my lover,
flowing gently over lips and teeth.
I belong to my lover,
and his desire is for me (7:6-10).

A final word is in order, albeit a potentially anticlimactic one. Obviously not everyone who reads this is married or ever will be. That is why I am gratified that the church throughout the centuries has been drawn to the allegorical interpretation of the Song of Songs. This is the reading of many of the mystics, and I believe it is a legitimate understanding, for surely we cannot exhaust the full meaning of Scripture with only the literal meaning.

In the allegorical, or mystical interpretation, we see the love relationship portrayed in the Song of Songs as a love relationship between God and man. As I have already suggested, it is a very small step to move from the intimate human-human relationship to the intimate human-divine relationship. So we may rightly regard this delightful love song as reflecting our relationship to Jesus Christ. Our devotional life can only be enriched as we think of our beloved Master when we say with the Song of Songs, "My beloved is mine and I am his" (2:16, RSV).

Questions for Review

1. Having read again (or for the first time) various portions of the Song of Songs, were you surprised that it is so explicit regarding marital sexual love?

2. Have you ever heard (or given) a sermon on the Song of Songs? Why is it that we tend to shy away from this book? Is your church being intentional about helping its young people to develop positive and healthy views about sex? Do you have programs to assist parents in educating their children in these matters?

3. Would you agree that the church and our society have been shortchanged by our neglect of this song?

4. Were you surprised by the results of the *Redbook* survey? Why do you think it is true that "religious women have more fun?" Is the fact that *trust* is a prerequisite to fulfillment a key factor?

5. Is there a correlation between the sacredness of sex and the enjoyment of sex? In light of the Song of Songs, this tandem ought to be proclaimed by the church as a strong and viable alternative to the twisted and distorted views propounded by an unenlightened society.

Seven

Isaiah Reclaims God's Authority

I want to introduce to you one of the pivotal figures in all of history, sacred or secular. He has left his mark on the Old Testament and is regarded as the greatest of the prophets. On the world stage, he was instrumental in the events which affected the nations. His stature is demonstrated in five major areas:

• His ideas of God constitute a high water mark in the theology of the Old Testament.

• His poetry has been hailed as the very best in all of literature. Its structure, parallelism, double entendre, chiasmus and other techniques convey a symmetry and beauty seldom equalled.

• He is a statesman of the first order. Of noble birth, he had easy access to kings and was their confidant. He developed a unique understanding of international diplomacy from a profound theological perspective. He was devout, cultured, reflective and brilliant.

• His influence has been far-reaching. The ideas of this one man, more than any other single individual from the Old

Testament, have shaped our Christian way of thinking. Except for the Psalms, Isaiah is the most frequently quoted book in the New Testament.

• Some of the greatest music of the ages has received its inspiration from Isaiah. George Frederick Handel's incomparable "Messiah" perennially lifts our spirits with these ancient words set to music: "O, Thou that tellest good tidings to Zion" (Isaiah 52:7) and "For unto us a child is born, unto us a Son is given" (Isaiah 9:6, KJV).

But that is not all—some of the greatest ideas of the ages find their origin or their finest expression in Isaiah.

The *holiness of God* is a major theme of this book. "Holy, holy, holy is the Lord Almighty; the whole earth is full of his glory," proclaimed the seraphim in Isaiah 6:3. The characteristic name for Isaiah's God is "Yahweh, the Holy One of Israel." No fewer than thirty times is the ascription "Holy One" or "Holy One of Israel" given to Yahweh. The holy character of all God's people is directly related to the holy character of the God whom they serve.

The idea of *God's pathos* is portrayed throughout. We see how God's heart is broken over his people's waywardness. God's judgments come, not because of a capricious anger, but begrudgingly and with painful reservation. God is quick to express compassion.

> For a brief moment I abandoned you,
> but with deep compassion I will bring you back.
> In a surge of anger I hid my face from you for a moment,
> but with everlasting kindness I will have compassion on you
> (Isaiah 54:7, 8).

The notion of *redemptive suffering* is nowhere more powerfully or more personally proclaimed than it is in Isaiah 53, the portrayal of the suffering servant. This is the original "wounded healer," to borrow a phrase from Henri Nouwen. Certainly the life of Jesus of Nazareth gave ultimate expression to the suffering of the servant on behalf of all humankind. May the church, the body of Christ, rediscover the same role for itself.

The prophet shares with us *hope*, a precious gift without which we simply could not continue. Hope is passed on from one generation to the next as people relate stories of their own restoration after an experience of devastation. Our own sense of hope for the future is given validity by the reality of hope fulfilled in the lives of our ancestors. Isaiah and the people of Israel are some of those ancestors, and their testimonies of hope have profoundly affected our own. Note, for example, these words:

> The people walking in darkness
> have seen a great light;
> on those living in the land of the shadow of death
> a light has dawned. . . .
> For to us a child is born, to us a son is given,
> and the government will be on his shoulders.
> And he will be called Wonderful Counselor,
> Mighty God, Everlasting Father, Prince of Peace
> (Isaiah 9:2, 6).

Or, take a lesser-known passage from Isaiah 25:6-9. Following the gloomy picture of darkness and destruction in chapter 24 comes this vision of hope. There will one day be a great feast on God's holy mountain. All nations will gather at this celebration of God's deliverance and restoration. The profundity of this hope knows no limits, for the author proclaims that the ultimate enemy of hope will be destroyed, for God "will swallow up death forever" (25:8).

Where did Paul the apostle get his profound notion of the hope of victory over death for the Christian? To be sure, it was from the reality of the resurrection of Jesus, but his greatest lyrical formulation of that hope is found in 1 Corinthians 15:54, "Death is swallowed up in victory" (RSV). It is a direct quotation of Isaiah 25:8 from the Septuagint, or Greek translation of the Old Testament.

Finally, one of the greatest expressions of hope is found in chapters 40-55. Jerusalem had been destroyed, the people were carried off to exile in Babylon and all had lost hope—except for one lonely prophet who remembered the character of God, what he had done in the past and what he could do in the present. This prophet was open to the Word of God which came to him saying, "Tell the people they are going home." It was such an unrealistic hope that no one believed the prophet. But God was true to his Word, and very soon these exiled citizens of Zion were returning home. As Isaiah 55:13 says, their return shall be "an everlasting sign [of hope] which will not be destroyed." And all who have faith to consider Israel's story as their own will find in this sign an eternal source of hope.

Who, then, is this remarkable individual, Isaiah, and what were the influences that shaped his life?

Use your imagination and travel back to the eighth century B.C. The country is Israel, the city is Jerusalem, and the man standing before you is Isaiah. But let's allow him to tell his own story.

The year was 760. My Father had just named me Isaiah, which means, "God will save," and I was dedicated in the temple.

My father was quite wealthy and influential in the city. Jerusalem was a wonderfully exciting place to be. We thought of it as the center of the earth. Certainly it was the center of all the cultural and intellectual activities.

Under the reign of King Uzziah, life was good. Not since the time of David and Solomon had we enjoyed such security, stability and prosperity. In 742 I had just turned 22. I was beginning to make it on my own, and the future seemed limitless. But unexpectedly King Uzziah died. Now tragedy and uncertainty had invaded my world.

Fearful and anxious about the future, I went to the temple that day in 742. There were others there worshiping God, each dealing with heavy concerns. Then it happened. I don't know about the others, but I felt the temple shake, and the room seemed to fill with smoke. When I looked up I saw the Lord sitting on a throne, majestic and regal—The King of Kings.

Then I knew the meaning of my vision: No matter who was the king of our country, there was only one ultimate King—God himself. He is the sovereign ruler over all the earth. All the nations of the world, Assyria, Egypt, Babylon or Israel, are simply God's instruments.

Then I heard a voice, incredibly loud, shouting, "Holy, holy, holy is the Lord of hosts; the whole earth is full of his glory." What an awesome experience it was to be in the presence of the holy King of the world.

There were some folks in my day who had grown accustomed to God, or to their picture of God. They had become too comfortable, and God had become a casual acquaintance. That is not the God I encountered in the temple. I was confronted with a God who is majestic—the hem of his royal robe filled the temple. I saw a God who is powerful—the seraphim, winged creatures, covered themselves. In neighboring Egypt the seraphim stretched out their wings to *protect* their king. But I saw that God's glory was so overwhelming that the seraphim had to cover themselves for their own protection. I saw a God whose mystery was shrouded in the smoke that filled the temple. The God I met that day left no mistake as to his character: "Holy, holy, holy is the Lord of hosts," the seraphim cried.

In the presence of the Pure One, the Holy One of Israel, I felt unworthy, human, finite, unclean. I cried out, "Woe is me, I am undone, I am a person of unclean lips and I dwell in the midst of a people of unclean lips." And one of the winged creatures flew to the fire that was used for sacrifices, took a burning coal, touched it to my lips and purged my sinfulness.

Then I heard the Lord say, "Whom shall I send, and who will go for us?" How else could I respond but to say, "Here am I, send me"? Considering the circumstances, I saw no other option. So it was that I assumed my role as a prophet. My task was simple, though difficult. I was to tell the people: "Repent or be destroyed." I had a feeling that I knew which choice they would make (Isaiah 6).

If only they would have realized God loved them, cared for them and wanted to bring them healing and wholeness, but they had so desperately lost their way. I told them:

> The ox knows his master,
> the donkey his owner's manager,
> but Israel does not know,
> my people do not understand (Isaiah 1:3).

So I pleaded with them,

> Come now, let us reason together,
> Though your sins are like scarlet,
> they shall be as white as snow;
> though they are red as crimson,
> they shall be like wool.
> If you are willing and obedient,
> you will eat the best from the land;
> but if you resist and rebel,
> you will be devoured by the sword (1:18-20).

But they would not listen. My beloved Jerusalem, once known as the faithful city, the joy of the earth, had become a harlot. Where righteousness once reigned, now treachery and thievery and corruption were in vogue.

What incredible pain and sorrow it brought to God. Like a mother hen he would have gathered his children, if only they would have come. Whatever judgment came against my country came reluctantly, begrudgingly, from the deeply sorrowing heart of God, not from vindictiveness.

You see, Israel was like a vineyard that God planted and cared for meticulously. He tilled the land, planted the choicest vines, watched over that vineyard with utmost care. He looked for it to yield sweet grapes, but it yielded wild, bitter grapes. God expected to reap justice, but found injustice; God wanted to find righteousness, but received unrighteousness from my people (see Isaiah 5:1-7)!

The downfall started with King Ahaz, about ten years

after Uzziah's death. Ahaz was afraid of the two kings of the little countries to our north. They threatened, and he shook in his boots. Think of it—Ahaz, king of Israel, whose God is the King of the world, petrified by two insignificant figures. So, rather than trust in God, he turned to the great empire, Assyria, for help and protection.

There was a price tag. We would be forced to accept their taxes, their gods and their ways. That was the beginning of the end: a simple act of distrust and disobedience. I suppose that is where most of our undoing begins.

I remember the day I confronted Ahaz about this. "Ahaz," I said, "do not be afraid of the kings of Syria and Ephraim to the north. They will not stand; they will not harm you. God will protect you. Do you see that young woman standing there? She will conceive and bear a child, and we will call his name Immanuel. Before the child is three years old, those two kings will have been destroyed and you will be safe. It will happen if you believe and trust God in it. But if you do not believe and trust, you and your people will be washed away in a flood of destruction.

"As I said, O King, the child's name will be Immanuel, which means 'God with us.' Indeed, God will be with us—for good, if you obey, but for destruction if you disobey! King Ahaz, if you will not stand firm in faith, you will not stand at all" (Isaiah 7:9).

That was in 734. Ahaz chose a simple act of disobedience; but oh, the awesome repercussions he suffered. The Assyrians, under Tiglath Pilezer, swept in with unbelievable destruction. They devastated the countries of Samaria and Syria. Because we were their "ally," they spared our land but imposed an internal devastation: we were required to adopt their unholy religion and ways.

What a people believes is so crucial to the way they behave! It wasn't long—just one generation—before these same "friends," the Assyrians, were ravaging our own land, and their king, Sennacherib, was perched on the outskirts of Jerusalem, ready to take the holy city. Our king,

Hezekiah, was frightened, but once again the Lord sent word to me that by a miraculous act, the vast Assyrian army would be dispersed. No one believed me, but indeed in the middle of the night a pestilence entered the army and ravaged them, so that they fled for their lives. Jerusalem was spared—for awhile (Isaiah 36-39).

The theological compromises, the sinful residue, the political alliances and the propensity to rely on humans rather than on God, all were taking their toll. I can still hear the thunderous hoof beats of the horses as, in 587, the vast Babylonian army, like a swarm of locusts, swept down and began to level Jerusalem.

There was my friend Eliezer's home and Joshua's family, his sons killed before my eyes. He watched his wife and daughters carted off, never to be seen again. The fires raged all over the city. The temple, the sacred place of God, was engulfed in flames. Finally, Jerusalem was leveled. Nebuchadnezzer's men spread salt all over the city and, as we were being led away from our home as slaves, he made the proclamation that this city, the city of God, would never be rebuilt—a preposterous idea, spoken by an infidel Babylonian whose ruined city to this day lies buried under innumerable acres of sand (2 Kings 25).

It may be difficult to believe, but during all this time of despair and devastation I never ceased to hope. I named one of my sons "Shear-jashub," which means "a remnant shall return." I knew that even though there would be destruction, God would never forsake his people. There would always be a remnant (Isaiah 7:3; 10:20-27).

I knew that even though our kings were often corrupt and would not rely on God, that God, the great King, would bring to earth a King like unto himself someday. I could see into the future (not exactly when) to a time when a child would be born, and the people would call his name, "Wonderful Counselor, Mighty God, Everlasting Father, Prince of Peace" (9:6).

It wasn't long after we had been dragged off to Babylon

that God spoke to me again. He said, "Start packing, you're going home." So I began to tell my fellow Hebrews this.

But they would not believe me. Some said, "God has forsaken us and forgotten us." Others said, "God is too weak and is incapable of coming to our aid."

This was more than I could tolerate, so I reminded them of the God whom I had seen in the temple:

> Who has measured the waters in the hollow of his hand,
> or with the breadth of his hand marked off the heavens?
> Who has held the dust of the earth in a basket,
> or weighed the mountains on the scales and the
> hills in a balance? . . .
> Whom did the Lord consult to enlighten him,
> and who taught him the right way?
> Who was it that taught him knowledge
> or showed him the path of understanding?
> Surely the nations are like a drop in a bucket;
> they are regarded as dust on the scales; . . .
> Lift your eyes and look to the heavens:
> Who created all these?
> He who brings out the starry host one by one,
> and calls them each by name. . . .
> He will not grow tired or weary
> and increases the power of the weak.
> Even youths grow tired and weary . . .
> and young men stumble and fall;
> but those who hope in the Lord will renew their strength.
> They will soar on wings like eagles;
> they will run and not grow weary,
> they will walk and not be faint (Isa. 40:12, 14-15, 26, 28-31).

It wasn't long afterwards that we headed home. It was a glorious day, and it seemed as if the hills were breaking out in singing and the tress were clapping their hands as we passed by (Isaiah 55:13).

The God whose majesty, power and sovereign authority Isaiah saw is the same God who rules today. Let us choose to submit our lives to the One whose preeminent authority is matched only by his limitless love.

Questions for Review

1. Look again at the four major ideas that originated with or were enhanced by Isaiah (God's holiness, God's pathos, redemptive suffering and hope). Reflect on them, giving special attention to the biblical references cited.

2. In the first-person portrayal of Isaiah, could you identify with Isaiah at any point? Have you ever felt as though you were in the presence of God? What was it like? Did you feel your own unworthiness?

3. Do you think it is possible that we have become too comfortable, too casual with God? If so, how might we regain a greater sense of God's holiness, power and might?

4. Some people would say that much of the popular religion of today is too subjective, too person-centered and too experience-oriented. They maintain that it does not lift up the great, objective characteristics of God. Do you agree or disagree?

5. In Isaiah's confrontation with Ahaz, he notes that Ahaz' "simple act of disobedience" had such awesome repercussions; it was the beginning of the downfall for the whole country. The biblical writers were convinced that each human act, each moral decision, had extensive implications. In a society that for the most part believes that "just this once," —a casual encounter, or a careless misdeed—really will not matter, is this message from Isaiah sorely needed? Why?

Eight

Job
Reestablishes
Hope

A few years ago I was working on my Ph.D. dissertation. A friend who had supported us extensively both emotionally and financially during those difficult years had urged me to use his computer with its word processor program. He had outgrown that particular model in his business, and he knew it would facilitate things for me. I was hesitant to try to learn some new paraphernalia at this stage of my doctoral program, but he was insistent and I began to see the advantages. Soon I was typing away.

One evening, caught up in the thrill of the progress I was making, I worked later and later into the night. At 2:00 a.m. I pushed two wrong buttons and completely lost the fifty pages I had just typed!

I heard of a man who worked five years on his dissertation. His office at the university was such a mess that he had scarcely any unoccupied space left to keep his manuscript. So when he completed the project he laid the text on his trash can as he left for home. The custodian came in that night and threw out all the trash. Yes, dissertation and all!

Rabbi Harold Kushner wrote a best-selling book entitled, *When Bad Things Happen To Good People.* The first chapter conveys powerfully the existential pathos out of which he writes. In explaining why he wrote the book, he tells of his son, Aaron, who at eight months strangely stopped gaining weight. At the age of one year his hair began to fall out. After numerous attempts at diagnosis they found a doctor in Boston who determined that Aaron had the uncommon illness known as progeria or "rapid aging disease." Little Aaron would never grow beyond three feet in height; he would have no hair on his head or body. He would look like a little old man and die in his early teens.

As Rabbi Kushner shared this story of his family's personal tragedy, he was flooded with letters from people who had experienced the common pain of a loss that defies understanding or meaning. His book was a best-seller because, regardless of the dimensions of the tragedy, the experience of loss and the ensuing questions are common to us all. We are helplessly inundated by a host of questions: How can this be fair? What did I do wrong that I brought this upon myself or my loved one? How can a loving God allow this to happen? Is God really all powerful? If so, then why didn't he prevent this?

Most, if not all, of the attempts to answer these questions are inadequate. Some attempts are more noble than others, but all fall short. Without justifying my view extensively, I must say that Kushner's book, popular and helpful though it is, is inadequate. He portrays so movingly the dilemma in which we find ourselves, but he reduces the possibilities for understanding God's actions to two, and we must choose *one*: *either* God is all-loving and not all-powerful *or* God is all-powerful and not all-loving. On the surface, Kushner's view makes sense, for if God were indeed both all-loving and all-powerful, then he would not allow such tragic things to happen.

But his formulation is a little too neat. He forces an impossible choice. Historically, the church has never seen fit to choose between God's omnipotence and God's love. The church has held to the belief that God is *both* all-loving and all-powerful. Despite the inherent tension in this view, I concur with the historical position of the church.

I suspect that Kushner's ironclad "either/or" choice is derivative, in part, from his orthodox Jewish faith, which does not accept the possibility of miracles or the resurrection. Without explaining all the problems or easing all the difficulties, these two phenomena strongly suggest that our view of the matter cannot be limited to the confines of this world. As such, we enter the realm of mystery, but in my view, mystery need not be feared or avoided.

Frequently we encounter other attempts to come to terms with human tragedy and loss. One common attempt in many religious circles is in my view terribly offensive. Let me illustrate from a real-life situation. A friend shared with me about a recent tragedy in his church. Jim, a member of their youth group, a superior high school student who was bright and handsome—a shining star—was coming home from baseball practice one night and was struck by a car and instantly killed. Of course his family was devastated, as was the entire church and community. The church was opened the following day for any of the young people who wanted to come and talk. The church was filled to overflowing.

In this setting one well-meaning person shared what in my view is a harmfully erroneous view of God. He said to several teens, "God was walking through the garden of life and was picking the most beautiful flowers, and he picked Jimmy for his heavenly bouquet."

There are hosts of people who have gone through life angry at God because someone convinced them that God had taken their mother, father, child or friend from them for some silly heavenly bouquet, or for some other reason. I would be angry too. Many people who are outside the church are there, not because they do not want to be Christians, but because of a distorted picture of God that had been inflicted upon them at an early age. They need to hear the words of Jesus from Matthew 18:14, " . . . your Father in heaven is not willing that any of these little ones should be lost."

Perhaps the best attempt (outside of Scripture) to come to terms with the notion of human tragedy and its implications for our understanding of God is to be found in Leslie Weatherhead's classic little book, *The Will of God*. He wisely circumvents Kushner's dilemma by positing three aspects of the will of God: *the intentional will of God* (God's original intention—it is always good); *the circumstantial will of God* (Fallen human nature and free choice result in circumstances God would not have chosen); and *the ultimate will of God* (Nothing can ultimately thwart the will of God. His belief in the resurrection allows him to transcend Kushner's view which is limited to this time and space for meaning).

These books are helpful, but the best approach in all of literature to the questions of human tragedy and loss is found in the book of Job. Its portrayal of devastating loss, critique of inadequate solutions and ultimate trust in the mystery of God have never been equalled. When life crashes in and hope is lost, how do you begin again? Where do you turn? You turn to Job.

Carlyle has called this, "the most wonderful poem of any age and language."[1] It is a divinely inspired work which speaks with sensitivity and profundity to our most basic and existential concerns. It is indeed a magnificent treasure; I pray that God might aid us in its rediscovery.

Job was a righteous man, blameless in every way. He feared God and distanced himself from evil. Job was also blessed with a large family: seven sons and three daughters. He was a wealthy man, with 7,000 sheep, 3,000 camels, 1,000 oxen and 500 donkeys. He was known as the greatest man of the East.

Job embodied perfectly the reigning theology of the ancient world, the idea that righteousness and wealth belonged together. If you lived right, God would bless you. Just look at Job and see how God has taken care of him, they would say. It is a tried and true teaching as old as Moses and his followers in the Deuteronomic school.

But wait, there is something uncomfortable about that philosophy. It may be tried and true ninety percent of the time. Righteousness and blessing may go together most of the time, but what about the ten percent slice of life when blessing does not follow righteousness, when tragedy comes to the righteous? What about Job? Did blessing always follow this righteous man? Let's turn the page to the next chapter in Job's life.

In five minutes Job's beautifully woven life came completely unravelled. One of his servants came running to his home and announced that foreign raiders had descended from the plains and had driven off the oxen and asses and killed all the servants, that he alone was left. Before he had finished speaking, a second servant came rushing in and described how lightning had fallen from heaven and killed all seven thousand sheep and all the servants except him. But there was more tragic news, for before this second scenario had been fully related, a third servant came and told how the Chaldeans had raided all the camels and killed all the servants except him. Scarcely had he finished when yet another servant appeared and related how a fierce *sirocco,* or windstorm, had destroyed the house in which Job's ten children were gathered, and they were all dead.

All that Job held precious had been taken from him. But with all of that, the tragic turn of events had not yet come to an end. Job was afflicted with grotesque bodily sores from head to foot. Finally, Job's only possible source of solace, his wife, turned against him with ridicule and mockery.

In spite of all of this, the Bible says that Job remained faithful to God.

Job had lost his children, his possessions and the love and understanding of his wife. But all was not lost, for he still had three friends: Eliphaz, Bildad and Zophar. He felt certain that he could count on their understanding and consolation. When the three "friends" arrived they did the best thing any friend could do in the face of tragedy: they sat quietly and said nothing (for seven days). If only they had had the good wisdom to keep silent, for when they spoke they only added to Job's misery.

You see, the three friends were speaking on the basis of the standard theology of their day: If you did what was right and were faithful to God, then good things would follow. But if you did something wrong, then bad things would follow. It was all too clear that something horrible had happened to Job; therefore, according to this neatly defined logic, Job had done something terribly wrong. They decided that they would help him discover what it was.

Chapter after chapter in the book of Job is given to exploring this truncated theological position. Job insists that he is innocent, that he has done nothing to deserve what has happened to him. And he prevails. Indeed one of the main reasons for the writing of the book of Job is to destroy this false understanding of God and the way God works.

The first thing, then, that the book of Job says to us is that *when life crashes in, don't lay blame.* Do not blame yourself for events beyond your control. It should be easy to do, but old ideas die slowly, and this is no exception. Let me ask you, what is your first reaction when something bad happens to you or to someone you love? Don't you ask, "What did I do wrong?"

Kushner relates a powerful story of a nineteen-year-old coed from his congregation who suddenly and inexplicably collapsed and died at her college. When he went to see her parents, the first thing they said to him was, "Oh, if only we had gone to the synagogue this past Friday." For some mysterious reason they were blaming themselves and their "lack of religious dedication" for their daughter's death.

I do the same thing. Not long ago I was involved in too many things, became tired and stressed and pulled out in front of an oncoming car. My front bumper was torn off. Fortunately no one was hurt, but my first thought was, "What have I done wrong?"

When a husband or wife walks out on a marriage the spouse who is left alone will come to me. The most frequent feeling is not anger but guilt! "What did I do wrong?" he or she asks guiltily. We can beat ourselves to death with this ill-conceived, unhealthy theology.

We learn a second important aspect from the book of Job: It is utterly honest. It admits that there are some things we cannot understand. By so doing, the book avoids the one-sided views we mentioned above, presenting a position that few other writings seem willing to take. On the one hand, it avoids the impossible dichotomy (which Kushner posits) of a God who is *either* all loving *or* all powerful, but who cannot be both. On the other hand, the book refuses to resort to the tidy, perhaps too tidy, delineation of the will of God suggested by Weatherhead.

Rather, the author of Job admits straight on that there are some things about the divine, eternal realm which we *cannot understand.* In my view, the pivotal passage in Job is chapter 28. It might be aptly titled, "Where may wisdom be found?" Here the author extols the *seemingly* limitless possibilities of human understanding. Human beings can do anything they make up their minds to do. They can go deep into the earth for precious metals and do things that once were thought impossible. But with all of our human accomplishments there still remains the haunting question, "But where can wisdom be found? Where does understanding dwell?" (Job 28:12). The author is correct when he writes in the following verse, "Man does not comprehend its worth, it cannot be found in the land of the living." Even though our human accomplishments are legion, we simply cannot fully understand the nature and ways of God.

"Where may wisdom be found?" The question remains unanswered and not by accident. Nor should its unanswerability be lost on us. We ought to recognize that in this life there are aspects of the human drama that we will never understand this side of heaven.

While chapter 28, with its eternal question mark, is the pivotal passage in the book of Job, it is not the final one. Yet to come is the enigmatic episode of the whirlwind (vv. 38-41). Out of the whirlwind God speaks to Job and touches his deepest need. This is the climax of the story, and it should not be missed. For as haunting as Job's questions were, they were not his ultimate concern. No, Job's deepest concern in the midst of his tremendous loss was "Have I lost God, too? Has God forsaken me? Does God no longer love me? Am I completely alone, cut off from the One who is dearer to me than life itself?"

Job looked around for some sign, any sign of God's presence. There was none. But wait. Look—out on the horizon is a slight wind. It is gathering steam and moving this way. Now it is a powerful whirlwind and is nearly upon us. And out of the whirlwind comes the voice of God! He *is* present. He *does* care. He has not abandoned me!

When our son and daughter were small they would run and play and eventually fall and scrape their knees. When they did, they would cry and instinctively run to Mommy. The world had been cruel to them. They were in pain. In the midst of the unkindness and pain they wanted to be reassured that the most important person in their lives still loved them. I suspect that when tragedy strikes us our deepest concern is that God still loves us despite the appearances of life. That is the message of Job.

Assured of that, we can move with renewed hope beyond the tragedy into new dimensions of living. May I share with you a story from my family? It is in some sense a tribute to my dad and to his courage and to the love and grace of God on whom he relied.

Our ancestors had settled in the Mingo valley in west central Ohio in the early 1800s. Dad's father moved to a neighboring farm which was owned by a relative. There in a big frame house on a hill, Dad was born in 1914. He was married in that house and spent most of his waking hours farming the 530 acres around it.

Six boys were born to him and my mother, and so Dad took one of the grain fields near the house and converted it into a baseball field. Our home was often the scene of Little League games, church youth group activities and community gatherings. In the winter we could be found ice skating on one of the four ponds or out sledding on the hills in the west pasture. Nearly every Sunday afternoon the basketball court in the barn was home for ten or fifteen of us.

We milked cows, made hay, plowed corn, built and mended fences and took sheep and hogs to the county fair. But most of all we created memories on that farm. On summer evenings we would sit and reflect under the big maple trees which rimmed our house. Later in the night we would play games such as kick-the-can or hide-and-seek, and then often we would sleep out under the heavens.

Dad did not own the farm; his cousin did. But since his cousin and his wife were unable to have children and because they were very much a part of our family, the cousin made it known to Dad that he had willed the farm to him.

A few years ago, while shoveling snow, the cousin died. His death seemed to twist something in his wife's spirit. She became an embittered recluse. In her bitterness she changed the will so that Dad would no longer inherit the farm. Like a modern-day Job, Dad had lost nearly everything dear to him. He had poured his life out into that soil and now it was gone.

Dad was distraught. He couldn't eat or sleep. His weight dropped and it looked as if he were going to die of a broken heart. All his questions of "Why?" remained unanswered.

But Dad must have seen his own whirlwind and heard a voice from God, because he caught hold of an idea. He decided to run for county commissioner. He had dabbled in politics much earlier in his life, but with six boys to rear he had to put politics on the back burner. But was it now too late? What if he lost, many of us wondered. Would this be the final blow of disappointment? He campaigned hard and won.

Then he had another dream. He would refurbish the original log cabin of his ancestors. He brought it up from the north pasture and rebuilt it. This past Thanksgiving, as he and Mom were sitting down alone for their mid-morning coffee, his six boys and their families, dressed as pilgrims and Indians, came to the cabin with Thanksgiving dinner in hand. They had much to be thankful for.

Yes, life had crashed in for a time; all seemed to have been lost. And there was the searching for meaning and understanding, but out of the tragedy came the affirmation of the unwavering love of God.

When life crashes in, how do you begin again? You cry and you agonize. You ask, "Why?" a thousand times and more, and then you hear a stirring, a movement in the wind. Even though you still do not understand, you know that God is there. He is with you and somehow his love will sustain you. Your hope will be renewed.

Questions for Review

1. Have you experienced times of loss and heartbreak? Try to remember what you felt, what thoughts went through your mind, what physical and emotional sensations you had.

2. Have you gone through part of your life angry at God because you believed God had taken a loved one from you? Do you know anyone who has felt this way? Do you suppose that if you were able to learn the background of some of your unchurched friends that you might find something like this that has kept them away from God all these years?

3. The ancient theology that "if you live a righteous life God will bless you" is still with us today. Can you think of examples? What is wrong with that as an ironclad view?

4. The converse of that view is still around today. Think back to the last time something bad happened. What was your first thought? For many of us it is, "What did I do wrong? Why is God punishing me?" What is wrong with this view?

5. I admire the book of Job because it *honestly* admits that there are some things which we cannot understand. How do you feel about that? Do you think it is an easy way out, or a realistic facing of reality? Read chapter 28 of Job again.

Nine

Proverbs Redirects Young People

The book of Proverbs is a training manual for life. Think about it: we train people how to be engineers, secretaries, lawyers, teachers and preachers. We do not send anyone into the operating room unless she has had prior medical training. In every walk of life we train people, except in the most basic area of daily living.

Whether or not it is asked openly, the underlying question that young people are wondering is, "How do I get along in the world?" The answer we give them is, "I don't know, you just do it." That has been the prevailing philosophy, and from the looks of our society I am not so sure how well this do-it-yourself approach to life is working. It reminds me of some of the do-it-yourself projects I have attempted around our house; their success is questionable at best. All of us need training and guidance.

Can you imagine trying to live life completely on your own as if you were the first person who ever lived? Of course this is so unrealistic it is almost impossible to imagine. We simply don't live that way. Every day we acknowledge our indebtedness to Edison when we turn on the light switch. Each day we build on the past achievements of folks such as Alexander Graham Bell or Henry Ford when we speak on the telephone or drive an automobile. People have gone before us, and we reap the benefits of their knowledge and creativity in the form of gadgets, appliances and conveniences.

But in the business of *living* we so often act like we are on our own, as if no one had ever lived before we came along. We see no wisdom to be had, no advice to be gained. Many of us have not yet discovered the book of Proverbs, the distilled, refined, fine-tuned wisdom of the ages—gems of wisdom that have been brightly polished in the sands of time.

The proverbs come from farmers, carpenters, blacksmiths, homemakers—people from every walk of life; people who have been where you and I are going. They have reflected on life. They have gained insight and understanding, and they have passed these on to the next generation. That generation has contributed to the next, with the refining process developing along the way. The final product is the book of Proverbs.

This is everyday stuff from everyday people. It is down-to-earth wisdom. Dare we say it—it is good old horse sense! It is like a road map that tells us how to get on in the world.

Not long ago I was speaking for a friend in Orlando, Florida. After the program I asked him how to get back to the East-West Expressway, so I could go home. He said, "Follow me until a certain point. From there you are on your own, but you will only need to make two turns. It is easy!" So I followed him and I did fine—until we got to the place where he waved goodbye and made a right turn. Now I was on my own. *Two turns, it's easy,* I said to myself. I got hopelessly lost!

It is awfully easy to get lost in completely new territory. That is precisely the difficult thing about being a young person moving into life—you are moving into a future that is completely unknown. That is why this book of Proverbs is so great. It is like having someone guide you through a strange and unknown city.

Don't you love it when you ask directions at a local gas station and the attendant tells you which way to go, but then adds those famous last words, "You can't miss it"? What he means is that *he* can't miss it because *he* has been there before. But *you* can miss it. Often our young people do too.

I was talking with a keen and insightful gentleman recently. We were discussing a particular aspect of a job he used to do. It was intricate work, and I commented on how difficult it was. His response was especially wise—very simple but especially wise: "Nothing is difficult if you know how to do it." Brilliant. Life isn't difficult—if you know how to do it. But the problem with life is that so much of it is new, especially the first twenty or so years.

Fortunately there are people who have gone before us, and they have left us some very sound advice! Their guidance has become the wisdom for all seasons. This book of Proverbs is the original self-help book, and it far surpasses its modern day counterparts for balance and realism. Let's listen to just a few of the wise sayings contained in this remarkable book.

> Wise men store up knowledge,
> but the mouth of a fool invites ruin (10:14).

Not only is this statement true, but it is also a helpful check to guard against meaningless prattle.

> He who heeds discipline shows the way to life,
> but whoever ignores correction leads others astray (10:17).

It would be so helpful during those adolescent years, when a young person is inexorably and rightly breaking away, to establish his or her independence if that young person would also, at the same time, be open to instruction. Receptivity to wise counsel and the establishment of one's independence are not mutually exclusive, contrary to popular belief. Rather, a willingness to accept sound instruction will make possible a healthy transition into real independence.

This is particularly true today. Years ago there were risks involved in moving from childhood to adulthood, but the dangers weren't as great. If one veered off the path, it wasn't too difficult to get back on. But today, with drugs and various forms of sexually transmitted disease, if you veer off the path it's like falling over the edge of the Grand Canyon. It is extremely difficult to recover.

> He who walks with the wise grows wise,
> but a companion of fools suffers harm (13:20).

It *does* matter what kind of company we keep. It *is* important who our friends are. We are influenced by them even more than we know. Young people must choose friends wisely. Parents must pray that God will bring their children the right kind of friends.

> A heart at peace gives life to the body,
> but envy rots the bones (14:30).
> Pleasant words are a honeycomb,
> sweet to the soul and healing to the bones (16:24).
> A cheerful heart is good medicine,
> but a crushed spirit dries up the bones (17:22).

The relationship between psychology and health could hardly be stated better. Our mental, emotional and spiritual lives radically affect our physical health. Norman Vincent Peale has tried to convince several generations of the truth of this. He has simply been reminding us of these very old "proverbial" truths.

> A gentle answer turns away wrath,
> but a harsh word stirs up anger (15:1).

Think about your last family argument. Did it become a shouting match? Did one harsh word lead to another, with the volume level rising with each angry word? How much better it would have been if someone could have given a *soft answer.*

Pride goes before destruction,
a haughty spirit before a fall (16:18).

Pride and arrogance are not only an affront to God, but they also have within them the seeds of their own demise.

If a man pays back evil for good,
evil will never leave his house (17:13).

This is an interesting twist on a similar teaching by Jesus in the Sermon on the Mount. We should not return evil with evil, not only because Jesus commanded us not to, but because such behavior is senseless. There is no stopping the evil; one evil act leads to another, ad infinitum.

The righteous man who walks in his integrity—
blessed are his sons after him (20:7, RSV).

There is *no* greater gift that parents can give their children than the gift of integrity. Webster defines integrity as "the quality or state of being complete or undivided . . . soundness." Possessions, wealth and athletic ability can be passing things, but integrity is a quality that will enable the possessor to meet life with confidence.

Finally, let me offer a proverb of my own, one that I believe captures the essence of all the proverbs in this extraordinary book:

The right way is the wise way,
It is the way that makes sense.

Contrary to the popular opinion of the twentieth century, the right way, which is God's way, really *does* make the best sense. It leads to the healthiest relationships and assures a sense of wholeness within the individual. God's way is the wise way. For the everyday, nitty-gritty decisions of life the wise choice is always the right choice.

Besides affording us the wisdom of generations gone before us, Proverbs conveys a *realistic appreciation of the world.* These proverbs help us feel at home in the world. While I agree with the sentiments of the old song that "this world is not my final home," I also am reminded of other great hymns of the church: "This is My Father's World" and "For the Beauty of the Earth." Sometimes people in the church seem so heavenly minded they make no earthly sense. Many of us grew up with ample teaching about the bliss of heaven and the strain and struggle of life here on earth. We probably have felt a little guilty about enjoying life here.

But it *is* our Father's world. God created it and called it good. Not only that, but God also put a part of himself into this world. God infused his creation with part of his character. That character is revealed in beauty, truth, order and reason; God painted himself into the portrait of the world. Just as every child is a revelation of the parents who gave that child life, so this world is a revelation of the God who created it.

Periodically people in the church become fascinated with Eastern religion. The thought of denying this world and going off to a barren mountain retreat to contemplate God seems somehow to capture the essence of true Christianity. But that is so completely contrary to our Judeo-Christian faith. Ours is not a religion that seeks escape from this world, nor does it despise this world. Far from it. It affirms this world. There is something about this world that as we contemplate it, moves us to respond with the songwriter who had tasted so deeply of the earth's riches: "How great thou art!"

Those farmers, carpenters and other homespun

philosophers responsible for the book of Proverbs, whom I mentioned at the beginning of this chapter, believed this about God and his world. They believed that if they observed this world carefully they could learn a great deal about God. This is called "natural theology." Sadly the Protestant church has disparaged natural theology for several decades for fear that an emphasis on it would take away from the better known "supernatural theology," which emphasizes God's special ways of relating to his people through saving acts.

The related phrase, "the acts of God," has been ubiquitous in circles of Old Testament theology. Certainly God's mighty acts need not be denied, but neither do they need to be emphasized to the point of excluding the quiet revelation of God through his creation.

Fortunately, through the efforts of Bernhard W. Anderson and others, the church is beginning once again to rediscover and appreciate the insights of natural theology. I suspect that if we had not neglected the book of Proverbs we would not have lost our way in this matter, for it is the most extensive depository of natural theology there is.

An additional benefit that would come to the church through rediscovering Proverbs is the gaining of some religious common sense. Is it an exaggeration to say that the religious world needs a healthy dose of this old fashioned remedy? As the church is increasingly affected by the phenomenon of television and accompanying claims for an electrifying, thrilling, miraculous, glitzy relationship with God, it is time to acclaim the virtues of down-to-earth, proverbial wisdom—religious common sense.

Do you ever have the feeling that one television evangelist is trying to outdo another in his or her claims for the supernatural activity of God? Do you ever wonder if there is a correlation between miracles claimed and money gained?

I suspect that this passion for phenomenal religion has made its way to where you and I live, the local church.

Many folks feel as though they are second-class Christians because they have not experienced and are not even comfortable with such ecstatic phenomena as they see on television. Their lives are not a steady stream of "miracles."

There is a humorous story about a man who dragged his reluctant wife on a hunting safari, much against her will. Deep into the bush country they set up their tent and made camp as he prepared to go hunting. On his way out, he gave his wife a bell and said, "If there is any danger, ring this bell and I'll come running back." She sat down with her knitting as he headed off in pursuit of wild animals. He had barely left camp when he heard the bell ringing. He came running back and said, "What's wrong, dear? Are you hurt or in danger?"

She said, "Oh no, I just wanted to see if it would work."

He said, "Only ring the bell if there is real danger and then I'll come." He headed off into the bush again. Fifteen minutes had passed when he heard the bell again and came running back to camp. "What's wrong dear? Are you okay?"

She said, "Oh yes, I just bumped the bell off the table, that's all. I'm fine."

He said, "Ring the bell *only* if you are in danger."

She said, "Okay."

He headed off into the bush a third time, hunted for awhile, heard the bell ringing again and came tearing back to camp. The place was in total disarray, the tent was in shreds, the food had been thrown all over the ground, his wife was wounded, and there were lion paw prints everywhere on the ground. He looked at the whole scene and said to his wife, "Well, that's more like it!"

It would appear that many in the religious community seem happy with their religious experience only when they create a disaster which in turn requires a "miraculous" work of God. They sit back and say, "Well, that's more like it." In this scheme of things, the only place God seems to be at work is in the spectacular.

As a young person I clearly remember wrestling with

the whole notion of evangelical Christianity. I believed in it intellectually, but the one major stumbling block for me was the people who were outspoken, obvious Christians who could talk about their faith at the drop of a hat, and usually did, but who lived lives that appeared disastrous. It didn't add up. They had no control over their children or were insensitive to their needs. There was little mutual understanding in their marriages. They seemed to do so many foolish things. And they seldom appreciated the classics, whether it be art, music or literature, which in my view reflected a lack of appreciation for the world.

I am not trying to be unkind, but these were the honest reflections of a young person. I suspect they are not too different from some of our young people's thoughts about "religion" today. But then I began to see that, while these people had had genuine experiences with God, they had failed to realize that successful daily living is determined largely by how well they mastered the natural laws which God put into his world: how to get along with people, how to discipline children, the use of one's time and money, the establishing of an effective work ethic, one's business dealings, virtues and values which are treasured and developed, how to deal with temptation, depression, anger. These are the Monday-through-Saturday matters of faith and living. These are the concerns of the book of Proverbs. When they are made a priority in living and then combined with a fervent, evangelical faith, then God's people will have the balance that I think he longs for them to have.

As I have suggested, the book of Proverbs was written primarily to help young people get along in the world, to pass on to the new generation the accumulated wisdom of previous generations. You will not find esoteric theology or ecstatic experiences, miracles or mysteries, burning bushes or visionary revelations, just solid values that have stood the test of time, the good sense often lacking in our time. Proverbs is a road map. If you follow its directions, you will arrive at your God-intended destination.

Questions for Review

1. The book of Proverbs comes from a different tradition in the Old Testament. It is known as the wisdom tradition, and it communicates its message in a way that is different from anything else we have discussed in this book. The focus of this tradition is on God's wise ways as they are revealed through the created order, i.e., through what one can observe by looking at creation and life in general. Think for a moment about your own wisdom tradition, and call to mind some proverbs that you grew up with. Do they ring true? Are they helpful guides for your life? How do they align with Scripture?

2. Sometimes people feel as though the Bible has such sacrosanct language that it can't really relate to everyday folks like us. Have you ever felt that way? Can you see why a book like Proverbs, the product of everyday people, would have a special appeal?

3. I take our confirmation class each year through a daily devotional journal based on the book of Proverbs. Does your church have a plan for acquainting its young people with this book which was written expressly for youth?

4. Have you ever been "so heavenly minded you were no earthly good"? Do you see how this view runs contrary to the philosophy of the book of Proverbs? Some churches and denominations pride themselves in the fact that they are "world-denying." Is this really a biblical ideal?

5. How do you feel about the comments in this chapter on the importance of religious common sense? Do we need more of it or less? Why?

Ten

Psalms Reflects Our Deep Feelings

He was one of the Soviet Union's most famous political prisoners, an outspoken dissident and a Jew. Anatoli Shcharansky had spent nine years in the Soviet Gulag, an extensive system of prison and work camps. Happily, on a cold day in February 1986, he found himself about to be released and extradited to Israel.

During the near decade of imprisonment, most of his possessions had been taken from him. But on that wintry day he clung to a miniature copy of the book of Psalms which his wife Avital had sent from Israel. It had come to mean so much to him that he once spent 130 days in solitary confinement because he refused to surrender it to the authorities.

On this, the day of his release, the Soviet guards tried again to take it. But Shcharansky defied their authority, threw himself into the snow and cried, "Not another step. I said I would not leave without the Psalms that have helped me so much." He was released as planned, with his book of Psalms.

Isn't it amazing, the power of words written on a page? Israel's Psalms were powerful enough to make a man prefer to stay in bondage *with* them rather than enter into freedom *without* them. I suspect that few of us have developed an appreciation for the book of Psalms equal to Shcharansky's, but his story demonstrates that it is possible.

I believe that the Psalms held such power for Shcharansky because they expressed the deepest feelings of his heart. They strike a nerve at a level far deeper than our cognitive powers can take us. They are like Paul's description of the Spirit in Romans 8.

> ... the Spirit helps us in our weakness. We do not know what we ought to pray for, but the Spirit himself intercedes for us with groans that words cannot express (v. 8:26).

It is no accident that the Psalms were written as poetry. There is something about poetry which gives special power to the ideas they frame. Carl Sandburg, the great literary figure and biographer of Lincoln, said that poetry is "an assault on the unintelligible." It has a unique capacity for expressing what we feel but find difficult to articulate. As such, it provides a frame of reference to our reality.

Part of the beauty of the Psalms is that they explore the whole gamut of human emotions, keeping step with the diversity as well as the depth of our feelings.

Take the feeling of *calmness*. When life is chaotic and nearly out of control, is there anything to compare with the soothing effect of the words of the 23rd Psalm?

> The Lord is my shepherd; I shall want.
> He maketh me to lie down in green pastures:
> he leadeth me beside the still waters.
> He restoreth my soul (vv. 1-3a, KJV).
> Surely goodness and mercy shall follow me
> all the days of my life:

and I will dwell in the house of the Lord for ever (v. 6, KJV).

There is a newly developing science of language called psycholinguistics which suggests that words carry a power beyond themselves. As I have seen a calm come over a person as the words of this great psalm are read, I find myself in agreement with the theory. I have experienced the same effect myself; I suspect you have as well.

Or consider the notion of *praise*. There is within all of us an innate need to offer praise. Whether we do it verbally, through our vocation, or in some other way, we find ourselves incomplete unless we acknowledge a Power, a Person, a Reality beyond ourselves. The last five psalms (146-150) are a testimony to this.

> Praise the Lord.
> How good it is to sing praises to our God,
> how pleasant and fitting to praise him! (147:1).

And the Psalter concludes appropriately:

> Let everything that has breath praise the Lord.
> Praise the Lord (150:6).

Do you suppose that our preoccupation with sports and movie celebrities in this country represents a misplaced expression of this inherent need to praise?

Think about the desire to *be known and understood*. Paul Tournier, eminent Swiss medical doctor and psychiatrist, has written a classic entitled, *To Understand Each Other*. Among the gems of wisdom in this little volume is this statement: "No one can find a full life without feeling understood by at least one person. Misunderstood he loses his self-confidence, he loses his faith in life, or even in God."[4]

I know of few things more painful than feeling misunderstood. One feels isolated, alone, cut off. I see it in marriages where two individuals who were intended to become one have become estranged, distant, lonely. I see it in the enormous distancing between parents and their children. In a study done not long ago with conflict-ridden families, teenagers were asked, "What are the five things you most want for your life?" In a different room the parents of these same teenagers were asked, "What are the five things you most want for your teenagers?" Remarkably, the answers were identical in all five instances!

Both groups had the same goals but the chasm of estrangement between them was nevertheless enormous. Why? I have a theory: When our children are young, they are so enjoyable—they are like absorbent sponges, soaking up all of our attention and affection. But soon they begin to develop minds of their own, which is good if they are ever going to become independent and healthy adults.

This development requires that the relationship move to a whole new level. The rules are now changed. It suddenly becomes a two-way situation, and it takes lots of work and energy for the parent to interact with this emerging person. It isn't easy to listen reflectively, creatively and caringly—to hear and understand. Some parents never make the transition. Later, when their children are fifteen or sixteen, even though they both may actually want the same things, emotionally they are miles apart, feeling mutually misunderstood and frustrated.

The paradigm for understanding is found in Psalm 139. Note the extent to which God goes to understand us.

O Lord, you have searched me and you know me.
You know when I sit and when I rise;
you perceive my thoughts from afar.
You discern my going out and my lying down;
you are familiar with all my ways.
Before a word is on my tongue
you know it completely, O Lord.
You hem me in—behind and before;
you have laid your hand upon me.
Such knowledge is too wonderful for me,
too lofty for me to attain (vv. 1-6).

In these six verses, note the subject, verb and object. God is the subject, I am the object and the verb is some form of the word, "to know, understand." In each verse the verbs are all active, energetic, exhausting terms. It takes effort to know and understand another person. God is intentional in doing that for us. God knows me; he understands me.

> Where can I go from your Spirit?
> Where can I flee from your presence?
> If I go up to the heavens, you are there;
> if I make my bed in the depths, you are there.
> If I rise on the wings of the dawn,
> if I settle on the far side of the sea,
> even there your hand will guide me,
> your right hand will hold me fast.
> If I say, "Surely the darkness will hide me
> and the light become night around me,"
> even the darkness will not be dark to you;
> the night will shine like the day,
> for darkness is as light to you (vv. 7-12).

In this second portion of the psalm the situation is reversed. I am the subject, God is the object and the verb is some form of the word, "to flee." The point is that you can not really flee from Someone who knows you and understands you.

> For you created my inmost being;
> you knit me together in my mother's womb.
> I praise you because I am fearfully and wonderfully made;
> your works are wonderful,
> I know that full well.
> My frame was not hidden from you
> when I was made in the secret place.
> When I was woven together in the depths of the earth,
> your eyes saw my unformed body.
> All the days ordained for me
> were written in your book
> before one of them came to be.
> How precious to me are your thoughts, O God!

How vast is the sum of them!
Were I to count them, they would outnumber
the grains of sand.
When I awake, I am still with you (vv. 13-18).

Finally, in the third section God is again the subject, I
am again the object, but now the verb is some form of the
word, "to create." The One who created me is the One who
understands me, and therefore there is no need to flee,
even if I could.

There is nothing else quite like the feeling of being
understood, and it is expressed nowhere more eloquently
than here in Psalm 139, unless it is in the *lived* expression
of understanding we give to those around us.

Consider the reality of *forgiveness*. I think a strong case
could be made that the word "forgiven" is the most wonderful word in the human language. Can you imagine what
life would be like without it? The sack filled with guilt that
Christian in *Pilgrim's Progress* carried on his back for so
much of his life would never have been dropped at the foot
of the cross to disappear down the hill into the empty tomb.
There would be no recourse, no starting over, no second
chance, no erasing the past.

I doubt there is a more poignant expression of our
heart's cry for forgiveness than what we find in Psalm 51.
Even though this psalm is the particular cry of a particular
person due to a particular event (David's plea for forgiveness after being confronted by the prophet Nathan about
his affair with Bathsheba), it has universal appeal and
application. We all have sinned and fallen short of the glory
of God. We all have violated our relationship with our
Creator. We all stand in need of God's mercy and grace.

Few of us can fully appreciate the depth of our need for
forgiveness unless and until we enter into the world of
Psalm 51.

Have mercy on me, O God,
according to your unfailing love;

according to your great compassion
blot out my transgressions.
Wash away all my iniquity
and cleanse me from my sin (vv. 1-2).

There is no notion of merit, of deserving God's favor. This is all grace and all mercy. And it is Old Testament! Where did we Christians get the mistaken notion that Jews believed they deserved God's favor? Where do we dare entertain the notion that the Old Testament is legalistic? This is a plea for mercy. Any and every act of forgiveness begins with the realization of our need for God's grace.

Nowhere else in the Scriptures is there such a *full-orbed* portrayal of forgiveness. We get snatches of what is involved in forgiveness from the New Testament, particularly the Gospels. The classic example is in John 8:1-11, the story of the woman taken in adultery. People are quick to point to Jesus' concluding words to the woman, "Neither do I condemn you; go, and do not sin again" (John 8:11, RSV), as an example of what it means to be forgiven. But so much more is unsaid. What are the inner thoughts and feelings of one who has been so graciously forgiven? We have no way of knowing from the passage in John's gospel.

But notice again the transparency of David in Psalm 51. The window to his inner self has been thrown open wide. We are invited in to understand and experience the subjective side of forgiveness. Note the verbs in 7-12:

Cleanse me with hyssop, and I will be clean;
wash me, and I will be whiter than snow.
Let me hear joy and gladness;
let the bones you have crushed rejoice.
Hide your face from my sins
and blot out all my iniquity.
Create in me a pure heart, O God,
and renew a steadfast spirit within me.
Do not cast me from your presence
or take your Holy Spirit from me.
Restore to me the joy of your salvation
and grant me a willing spirit, to sustain me.

There is a plea for cleansing, for washing, for the removal of sins, for a clean heart. Then come the next steps of restoration: a new spirit, a renewed joy. This inner experience is followed by an outer expression of thanksgiving and gratitude.

Then I will teach transgressors your ways,
and sinners will turn back to you.
O Lord, open my lips,
and my mouth will declare your praise (Psalm 51:13,15).

Forgiveness. Its origin may always remain a mystery in the heart of God, but its reality has never been more powerfully expressed than in this psalm, Psalm 51.

There are numerous other human emotions which are given expression in the Psalms.

• *Thanksgiving,* in psalms such as 136 and 138, "Give thanks to the Lord, for he is good. *His love endures forever*" (136:1).
• *Communion with God,* in Psalm 42, "As the deer pants for streams of water, so my soul pants for you, O God" (v. 1).
• *Trust,* in Psalm 37, "Trust in the Lord and do good; dwell in the land and enjoy safe pasture. Commit your way to the Lord; trust in him and he will do this" (vv. 3, 5).

But we have not yet touched on the theme which is the subject of the majority of the psalms: lament. We are accustomed, when we consider the Psalms, to think of praise, thanksgiving, joy and blessing. But most of the psalms do not deal with these themes at all; more are given to laments—deep and anguished expressions of grief, despair, loss and anger—than to any other single theme.

That is as it should be, for the deepest, most penetrating feelings we know are precisely these. We can handle our feelings of joy and happiness. But when our child is taken from us in a senseless accident, or our husband of forty years is slowly consumed by cancer, or our home with all of our memories is burned to the ground, we find it very difficult to carry on. When we don't know where to turn, we turn to the Psalms. They express what we are experiencing deep inside.

Doesn't Psalm 22 say exactly what you've felt but were afraid to say? Go ahead, turn to it as Jesus did when he was on the cross.

> My God, my God, why have you forsaken me?
> Why are you so far from saving me,
> so far from the words of my groaning?
> O my God, I cry out by day, but you do not answer,
> by night, and am not silent (vv. 1-2).

If we are honest, we all have felt this way. We are in excellent company. The beauty of this psalm is that it tells us that it is okay to feel that way. Lament is normal.

Note which psalm follows Psalm 22. I suspect the sequence was not an accident. Sometimes in our pain we need to cry out in the lament of Psalm 22 before God can lead us beside the still waters of Psalm 23.

If religion does not intersect life at these moments of lament and grief, then it isn't worth much at all. It doesn't need to *answer* the deep questions of grief, for I suspect there are no final answers this side of eternity (see discussion of the book of Job), but it needs to acknowledge them and feel the pathos with the one who is going through the valley of death.

The psalms of lament do this. They express what we are feeling but aren't sure how to say it, or are afraid to say it, for fear of the language we might use. Parenthetically, let me say that the New Testament contains nothing like the psalms of lament. For those who say that the New Testament is totally sufficient, that we no longer need the Old Testament, I bid them search through the New Testament for expressions of grief and pain!

I once heard a wise old preacher say that he had gone through three stages in his ministry. In the first stage he was an observer on the bank of a slow-moving river. His people were in the river and he saw it as his job to shout words of encouragement and instruction to the swimmers as they went by. In the second stage he discovered that he had to become more involved, so occasionally when someone was in trouble he would run down to the river, jump in and save the person from drowning.

Then the preacher was diagnosed as having a terminal illness. He had suddenly entered stage three. Now he was right there in the river with his folks, working together to survive. The psalms of lament were written by people and for people who are fully in the flow of the rivers of life.

Not long ago Elie Wiesel, survivor of concentration camps, was awarded the Nobel Peace prize. His father and mother and sister were murdered at Buchenwald. He decided that he would keep their memory alive, so he became a writer, a prolific and profound writer. When he was interviewed in New York, he said this:

> I still do not understand why God allowed the Holocaust to occur. I've had moments of anger and protest . . . But . . . I never left God, although He may have left me. Nor can I understand the silence or the eclipse of God in years when we needed Him most. But that does not push me farther away from Him. I would say that sometimes I have been closer to Him for that reason.

Elie Wiesel is a wonderful storyteller. Here is a story heard in the concentration camp: Three rabbis were putting God on trial and found him guilty as charged. When the trial ended, one rabbi looked at his watch and said, "It's time for prayers."

Our laments, like those of the psalmist, are the honest expressions of the deepest feelings of our beings. It has been my experience that you only express those kinds of feelings to Someone of whose love and constancy you are certain.

Questions for Review

1. Do you ever wish that you had the same strong attachment to the book of Psalms that Anatoli Shcharansky had? How does that develop? Does it come with age? Is there a certain amount of suffering that one must first experience? How can we deepen our spiritual sensitivities?

2. Turn again to Psalm 139. Sense again the lengths to which God has gone so that you might be known and understood. Are you able to draw upon that relationship in order to extend a similar understanding and knowledge to someone else?

3. Meditate a few moments on what it would be like if there were no such thing as forgiveness. Imagine how different your world would be. Is forgiveness an easy matter? How could anyone who has ever traversed the ground of Psalm 51 suggest such a thing?

4. Have you ever felt like crying out to/at God in grief, anger, pain, despair? Most of us have, and we are in good company—the company of the psalmist. Why might it be a healthy thing to express those feelings? Does the expression help you then to move on to an expression of trust?

5. Summarize what you feel is the greatest value of the Psalms for you.

Epilogue

Mark Trotter, senior minister of First United Methodist Church in San Diego, California tells a wonderful story about a bat mitzvah he attended. It was for the daughter of a rabbi friend of his. It was time for Robin to accept the duties of adulthood.

As part of the service, her uncle, also a rabbi, asked the family to come up to the Ark. He took out the Torah, written on two large scrolls. As he held it up he said, "I want to give a midrash on the Sinai story. When God gave the Torah on Mount Sinai, he said to Moses, 'Now bring me some guarantors, some people who will guarantee that the law will be preserved and kept alive.' Moses said, 'I will bring you the priests and the elders.' God said, 'No, not the priests and the elders.' Moses said, 'Then I will bring you the prophets.' God said, 'No, not the prophets.' Moses said, 'Then I will bring you the children.' God said, 'Yes'."

Then the rabbi took the Torah in his arms and handed it to Robin's grandparents. Her grandparents handed it to their children, Robin's parents. They handed it to Robin.

That is a real life parable. Similarly God intends for us to keep the story alive. Throughout the centuries the story of our faith has been passed down from generation to generation. We are what we are because people before us have been guarantors, good stewards of the Word.

I have a fear that this preservation of our heritage is in danger. Few in the church pass the story on. Those who do, often are transmitting only part of the story, the New Testament. The Old Testament, the sacred Scriptures of the early church, has been neglected by the modern church, and this at a time when the Jewish people are rediscovering and reclaiming their religious heritage with great enthusiasm.

If you have ever been present at a celebration of Passover, you will remember that at a certain point in the service one of the young boys will ask his father, "Why do we do this?" The father will respond, "We do this each year so that we will never forget that once we were slaves in Egypt, but now we are free."

"So that we will never forget"—I retell these stories from our Old Testament story of faith so that we in the church will never forget. I retell them with the hope that readers will be drawn back into the sacred Book and will rediscover the Story which shaped a people and which will continue to do so. I retell them with the conviction that God's message to Hosea, Ruth, Esther, Isaiah and the rest has something vital and essential to say to us. I retell them believing that our society needs to hear the serendipitous song of the Song of Songs, the word of hope in Job and the guiding, practical wisdom of Proverbs. I retell them because some have lost their way, detoured by doubt and despair—they need to hear the word of Ecclesiastes. Those who feel things too deep for words also need the book of Psalms, which reflects so profoundly those innermost emotions.

When Mel Fisher first discovered the ship Atocha and its treasure, he knew that he had made a remarkable find. Only after he began to examine the treasure more carefully did he realize that it far exceeded his expectations.

It is my prayer and hope that this attempt to help you rediscover the neglected treasure of the Old Testament will lead you into a fruitful searching of its riches. May you be a guarantor to those who come after you, preserving the heritage and passing it on to those whose lives it will shape with beauty and integrity.

Notes

1. C. S. Lewis, *Reflections On The Psalms*, (New York: Harcourt, Brace and World, 1958).

2. J. W. Hamilton, *What About Tomorrow?*, (New Jersey: Fleming H. Revell Co., 1972), 163, 164. Current copyright by Florence Hamilton. Used by permission.

3. J. A. Blevins, "Words," from *Living With Children*, October-December, 1981. ©1981 The Sunday School Board of the Southern Baptist Convention. All rights reserved. Used by permission.

4. P. Tournier, *To Understand Each Other*, (Atlanta: John Knox Press, 1967), inside cover.